Abused

CW01496710

Be Vigilant

**Eight more stories
of children murdered by
their parents or caregivers**

Jessica Jackson

This work is based on real cases
*The first part of each story is semi-fictionalised,
with some events and dialogue added*

*The second part tells the facts of each case,
detailing the injuries, trials and sentencing*

For the purposes of anonymity, names of siblings and friends have been changed unless where commonly known

*Cover photograph of
Charmaine West*

Contents

Hello Again

I know my books aren't for everyone, so thank you so much for picking up my 2nd book telling the stories of children murdered by their caregivers. Most of my friends can't read them – so I'm honoured that you are reading these stories, and I hope you'll 'enjoy' the book.

> If you can spare a moment when you've finished reading, I'd be very grateful if you'd help me to raise awareness of child abuse by rating or reviewing this book.

I also have a FREE e-book for you.

You can check it out overleaf …

Your Free E-Book

Exclusive only to my readers

**The tragic case
of Isaiah Torres**

*(with bonus content about
Baby Brianna Lopez)*

I'll let you know how to get your copy later

*(Royalties from my books go to
NSPCC, UNICEF and
Prevent Child Abuse America)*

Because She Loves You

(I apologise for using the racial slurs that were commonplace in 1970's UK)

BECAUSE OF WHAT CAME AFTER, when they hung young women upside down in their cellar, and tortured them to death, you probably know more about my step-parents than I ever did. My step-parents; the worst pair of serial killers in UK history. I'm sure you've read about them.

I was only six years old, and my little sister Anna was five, when our stepmother came into our lives. A beautiful young girl with big brown eyes, and the temper of the devil.

But before all that, things were different; when Anna and me had a real mother.

ONE SUNNY DAY in May, all three of us run out of the shop, with Mr Stewart close behind us.

'I'll come back and pay tomorrow,' calls Mam over her shoulder, as she pushes us down the street.

'Aye, you'd better,' shouts Mr Stewart. 'Or I'll get the boys in blue onto you.'

Anna grabs our mother's sleeve.

'Oh, don't worry, Anna. He always says that. But he knows I'll pay. Come on, who wants to play on the swings?'

The park isn't far away, and I'm soon running around, with Anna following behind. She's too scared to go down the slide, so I give her a little push at the top, and Mam catches her at the bottom.

'See, Anna! See! There's nothing to be scared of!' And I run back up the steps for my next turn. And the next. And the next.

When I see Mammy and Anna opening the shopping bag, I go and join them on the seat.

Mammy laughs. 'Hair dye, spaghetti hoops, and ciggies. All the essentials!'

'Didn't we get any sweets, Mam?'

'Not today, Char. But when my giro comes tomorrow.'

'Come on then, Anna,' I say. 'Let's have a go on the swings.'

Mammy pushes each of us in turn until she starts to look tired. 'It's time to go, girls.'

'Just a few more minutes, Mam.'

She shakes her head and smiles. 'You can always get round me, Char. Give Anna a push while I sit down and have another cig.'

'And can we come back tomorrow?'

She laughs, and ruffles my hair. 'What am I going to do with you? But we'll see. Now go and play; you've got five minutes.'

When we get back to the flat, Anna's Daddy is there. His bristles hurt my face.

Mam isn't happy to see him either. 'What the hell are you doing here?'

'Obvious, in't it? I want to see my daughter.' Anna's Daddy is from England, and he talks funny.

'Well, you've no right to see her.'

Anna and me play in the corner with our Tiny Tears. (Anna doesn't know she's not a real one, and that Mam got her on Glasgow market.)

After a few minutes, the grown-ups stop shouting and begin to talk normally. Before long, Anna's Daddy is taking Mammy's clothes off.

'The kids, you maniac!'

'Never mind about them; they need to know all about it anyway. It's time they learnt what Mammies and Daddies do.'

'They're just kids, Fred.'

'Still got to learn, Rena.'

Anna and me turn away. I wish we had some more toys to play with, but I make up a clapping game, and Anna smiles for the first time since her daddy arrived.

"What Mammies and Daddies do" ends with a few slaps and even a punch or two, then they both have a cigarette.

'Want one, Char?' says Anna's Daddy.

'No, I bloody well don't!'

'Cheeky madam. I'll soon knock some sense into her.'

'Oh no, you won't. She's mine. She's not yours.'

'Well, I know that! But my Anna's too good. She's no fun. Just does as she's told.'

'Leave them alone. Both of them.'

He shrugs. 'You coming down to Gloucester then, Rena?'

'I'd rather stay here. The kids are going to school now.'

'I can teach them more than they'll ever learn in school.'

He's stroking Mammy's legs. At the top. 'Been with any more Pakis lately?' He nods over at me.

'Of course not, you idiot!'

Anna's Daddy's face seems to go black. 'What the hell did you just call me?'

'Oh, I don't know. Does it matter?'

'Yes, it matters.' His hand has gone from her thigh to her neck. 'Now, what was it?'

I jump up. 'You leave my mammy alone.'

He whacks me in the mouth, but I don't stop. 'You're hurting her.'

'It's alright, Char,' Mammy wheezes. 'I'm okay.'

'What … did … you … call … me?'

'I can't remember.'

'Well, remember this.' And he punches her so hard she falls to the floor and he kicks her.

'Not the face! Not the face! I was going to go out tonight.'

'Huh! You never earn much anyway.' He aims a kick between her legs. 'Now, don't ever call me an idiot again. Got it?'

Mammy's lip is bleeding. 'Yeah, I've got it, Fred.'

'Now, clean yourself up and get out to work. There must be someone in Glasgow daft enough to have you.'

MAMMY LOOKS BEAUTIFUL. And although I think she'll be cold in that short skirt, I love the ways it fits her so neatly.

'Can I come out with you, Mam?'

She smiles and shakes her head. 'No, Char, I'm sorry. I'll be back soon, girls. Go to bed at half past.'

As soon as Mammy goes out, Anna's Daddy goes out too, but he comes back a few minutes later with two girls. They look just a few years older than me.

'Here they are,' he says to the girls, pointing at Anna and me.

'Aww, they're gorgeous,' says one of the girls, coming towards me. 'Is this one half Paki?'

'Yeah,' says Fred. 'Pretty though, isn't she?'

'How old are they?'

'The Paki one's six, and Anna's five.' He squeezes her shoulder. 'Anyway, never mind all that, let's get down to it.'

'Down to what?' says the second girl.

'What you came for.' And Fred starts touching the girls up their skirts, and one of them says she wants to go home. I hear him telling her not to be so bloody silly as I try to sneak Anna out of the room.

'Where do you think you're going?' says Fred. 'Stay and watch.'

'We're tired, Daddy,' says Anna. 'Can we go to bed?'

'Stay here. You'll learn something.'

So we come back and sit side by side in our usual corner as Anna's Daddy hurts the two girls.

'Open your eyes, Anna. Char, are you watching?'

'Pretend there's a curtain in front of us,' I whisper to Anna.

One of the girls screams. I jump up and kick Fred's legs. He doesn't stop; not even for a second. He just reaches round and throws me to one side.

'You watching, you kids? This is what Daddies do to their little girls, too. Be your turn in a year or two.'

'Don't listen,' I whisper to Anna again. 'Make yourself go cross-eyed and you won't have to see.'

We put our fingers in our ears until it's over. The girls are bleeding down their legs.

'And don't say nothing about this,' says Fred, looking first at the sobbing girls and then at us. 'Nobody's gonna believe you.'

As the girls leave, he clouts me for not watching closely enough, and makes us both look at the saggy thing between his legs. 'Get to bed, then,' he says. 'Night-night.'

I cuddle Anna, but she's shaking and crying. 'Shh, pet. It'll be alright.'

'He hurt those girls, Char.'

'I know. I know.'

'One day he's going to hurt me like that.'

I pretend to laugh. 'Oh yeah. I can just see Mammy letting him do that to you!'

'No, no she won't, will she? I hope she doesn't go away again.'

'Even if she does, we'll just go into care again. That last home was nice.'

I stroke her hair, and she eventually stops shaking.

It's a lot later when Mammy's key turns in the door. We hear her and Fred mumbling at each other, but there's not much shouting. Mammy comes in and watches us both for a few minutes, then kisses our foreheads. 'My girls,' I hear her say before she creeps out, whispering that we can have the new shoes we need. And sweets.

WE'VE HAD TO COME to Gloucester to live with Anna's Daddy. We're not sure why. Mammy didn't come with us, and we miss her, but it's not as bad as we thought it would be. Anna's Daddy is always out working, and he's quite nice to us when he's at home.

We're living on a caravan park out in the country, so we can see sheep and cows when we look out of the windows. Fred doesn't like us to go outside much though, and when he goes out, he usually locks the door and takes the key with him.

One day, Anna's Daddy brings a girl with him to the caravan. She's so pretty, with dark hair and big brown eyes, and she's wearing a lace dress and a fur coat. Fred introduces us just like he did with the girls back in Scotland, but this time, the girl seems happy, and when she gives a rag doll each to me and Anna we can't believe it.

'Oh my God,' she says, the first time she hears me speak. 'She's got a Scottish accent!'

'Of course I have!' I scowl at her. 'I was born in Coatbridge. Same as my mam. Same as Anna.'

'It's just … well, she's a Paki, isn't she Fred? It sounds so funny.'

'That Rena,' says Anna's Daddy, laughing. 'She'd go with anyone.'

'Aww, I didn't mean anything by it, Charmaine,' says the girl, stroking my arm.

And so I stop glaring at her and smile. 'I know you didn't. It's alright.'

We have a big meal together of sausage, egg, beans and chips, and Fred tells us Rose is his new girlfriend (even though he's still married to Mammy). Anna just accepts it, but of course I ask questions, and Fred tells me to shut up.

'I love kids,' she says to Anna and me. 'I want a big family of my own. They'll be your brothers and sisters.' She doesn't really look old enough to be talking like that, but she says it kindly, and I'm glad she likes kids.

A FEW DAYS LATER, when we're in town with Rose, some boys start following us down the street, and calling out, 'Dozy Rosie. Hey, Dozy Rosie, heard you've got yourself a gypsy boyfriend!'

'At least the fellas of Bishop's Cleve'll be safe for a while!' says a boy with greasy blond hair.

'Leave her alone,' I shout.

'My Fred'll have you,' she yells at them.

'Freddie West! Couldn't fight his way out of a paper bag!'

'Come on, girls.' She hurries us along and the boys soon give up.

'You're a good girl, Charmaine. Thanks for sticking up for me.'

Most nights, Rosie brings home lovely treats from the bakery where she works. Neither me nor Anna have tasted anything like them before. Pink meringues and chocolate eclairs and currant slices and Eccles cakes.

'These are lovely,' says Fred, spitting crumbs everywhere. 'But you're not going to work there anymore, my girl. I want you here all the time.'

'What about my wage, Fred? Mum and Dad still expect me to bring my pay packet home every week.'

'I'll pay you just the same. And I'm sick of you going back to them all the time. It's time you lived here properly.'

Rose looks like the cat that got the cream and found a little fish swimming around in the bottom of the dish. 'I'll be a good mum to these two, Fred.'

'I know you will, my little housewife. Pass me another currant slice.'

MISS FLETT HURRIES out of the school gates. 'You two still here?' She's going home herself; it must be really late.

'Rose won't be long, Miss.'

'This is the 3rd time this week. Tell your step-mum I have a couple of phone numbers of girls who'd be happy to pick you up when she can't manage it.'

'We'll tell her, Miss.'

We decide to walk home on our own; it's not far.

Rosie is waving goodbye to a man when we get there. 'Oh, it's you two! Is it that time already?'

'Miss Flett said she can give you the phone numbers of two girls who could meet us at the gates when you're busy.'

'She said what?'

'That if you wanted to, you could have their numbers.'

'Bloody cheek of that woman! We can sort this out between ourselves! We don't need anyone else coming and poking their nose in. Who do they think they are?'

'Yeah, okay Rose. It was just a couple of phone numbers. I didn't mean to start a riot.'

'Well, you bloody well *have* started one.'

I shrug. I don't get what she's so annoyed about.

'It's not often I get mad. But this has really made me furious.'

Anna and me look at each other.

'They weren't going to push in, Rosie. It was just that if you wanted their numbers, you could have them. Miss Flett was trying to be helpful.'

'Oh shut up! Look at the trouble you've caused. You'll be recruiting half the town next.'

I realise there's no chance of making sense of it, so for once I decide to be quiet.

'Pass me the scrubbing brush; I'll make a start on this floor.' And she scrubs vigorously, as if she could scrub her anger away. 'Get out of my sight, you two. Wait till your dad hears about this.'

I'm relieved when we hear Fred clanking up the path with his tools. He's got his faults, but I know he'll understand that Anna and me didn't do anything wrong.

Rose drops the scrubbing brush and starts at him the moment the door opens. 'This little madam has been going round recruiting people to pick them up from school!'

Anna's dad looks puzzled.

I decide to give it a try. 'I didn't, Fred. She's been bullying us. Making out we did something wrong.'

His expression changes. 'No bullies here, Charmaine,' he says quietly, and I realise that whatever he might really think, he's going to take her side, no matter what. I glance at Anna. She looks away.

'Alright, Rosie love?' And Fred grabs her in a hug, shooing us out of the way.

THAT WAS THE FIRST TIME I'd seen Rose lose her rag over nothing, and it made Anna nervous of saying the slightest thing in case it set her off. Anna spent days trying to understand it, but of course, I couldn't keep my big mouth shut.

'Were you really mad at me the other day, Rose?'

'Don't be so damn cheeky. You know I was.'

'But I only said Miss Flett could give you two phone numbers.'

'Don't start with me again, lady. Or you'll be sorry.' And I could tell by the look on her face it was time to let it go.

'Can I have a biscuit please, Rosie?'

'How many times, Charmaine? It's not Rosie, it's Mum.'

'But you're not my mam, or my mum, or whatever you call it down here.'

'I'm more of a mum to you than she'll ever be, now say it.'

'Rosie.'

'It's Mum. Now say it.'

'Rosie. I've got a real mam. Her name is Rena.'

She sighs and slaps my face.

19

'No tea for you tonight.'

'Why not? I'm really hungry.'

'Well, I'll think about it. But you've got to learn to stop being so bloody cheeky.'

'Fred wouldn't have stopped me from having enough to eat.'

Whack. 'Shut your mouth. And get to bed. Definitely no tea for you.'

WE'RE ON OUR WAY back from town, and the boys in the street are shouting at Rose again, so I reach for her hand to show her I care about her, but she whips it away.

'Get off, you dirty Paki.'

'But they were being horrible to you.'

She slaps my face.

'Ow!' I know I should shut my big mouth but I've never been very good at that. 'And why did you call me a Paki?'

'Cos that's what you are, you little bastard.'

Anna touches my arm and shakes her head. It's time to let it go. She's a year younger than me, but she's clever.

Later, in bed, I ask Anna if she knows what Rosie meant.

'I heard them talking about your dad once.'

'Oh yeah?'

'They said he was a taxi driver or a bus driver or something.'

I nod. Mammy had always told me he was rich and was going to come and look after us one day, but I'd also heard he was a bus driver too.

'So that's why, Char.'

It takes a minute for it to sink in. Almost all the bus drivers I've ever seen have beautiful brown skin. A bit like mine. 'I wish I could meet him, Anna.'

Anna squeezes my hand. 'It's funny; Rosie has lots of friends with dark skin, so I don't know why she called you a nasty name.'

Grown-ups are so complicated.

'I miss Mammy,' says Anna.

'Me too.'

LATELY, ROSIE HAS STARTED to call me a little bitch.

'It's Char-maine,' I say.

'Shut your mouth, bitch. Get up on that stool.'

'What for?'

'Get up there, Char-maine!'

So I have to climb up, and she grabs a piece of rope and ties my hands behind my back and then reaches for the wooden spoon. It hurts a lot, but I don't let her win; I keep my tears inside.

I tell Fred when he gets in from work, but as usual, he just laughs. 'Oh yeah. Look, there's some bruises coming out. Here, I'll rub them better.'

'They're not *that* high up!'

'Shut up, Char. They're all over. And don't be telling tales on Rosie. She's in charge when I'm not here.'

'She's not my mammy.'

Fred laughs again. 'We're in charge, Charmaine. Get used to it.'

I open my mouth to speak again, but Anna is shaking her head.

'Go outside and play,' says Fred. 'We'll call you when it's time for tea.'

'You need to keep quiet,' says Anna, as we take turns with the skipping rope. 'You'll be in serious trouble if you don't.'

'But they shouldn't boss us around so much, and she's not *your* mammy either.'

'I know. I miss our mam, Char. I wish she'd come and get us.'

'Me too.' As I pass her the rope I grab her and give her a cuddle. 'I'm glad we're sisters, Anna. We've always got each other to talk to when they're horrible to us.'

'Do you sometimes feel scared of them, Char?'

'Of them two? Of course not!' I am though. But I have to be strong for Anna.

'Just be a bit more careful. Please.'

'I'll try.' And I mean it, at the time. For Anna's sake, I *will* try.

FRED HAS BEEN 'AWAY' for a long time. Weeks and weeks. Anna cries herself to sleep at night because it seems ages since our mammy has been to see us as well, and we have to stay in this horrible caravan all the time, apart from when we're at school. We both like school and we even have a couple of friends, but when I try talking to some girls whose skin's almost the same colour as mine, with their colourful clothes and shining hair, they don't seem to want anything to do with plain little old me.

I concentrate hard in class. I want to be a teacher like Miss Symonds. She's the only teacher that smiles at me and she once asked me if I was alright. I gave her a big grin and told her I was great. If Rosie knew I'd spoken to anyone she'd kill me. Rosie's starting to remind me of the wicked stepmother I've been reading about at school.

MAMMY'S BEEN TO SEE US and she brought her new boyfriend! He's called John, and I really like him. Anna does too. He calls me the gap-tooth-fairy, because where my baby teeth have gone at the front, my big teeth haven't come through yet. It makes me giggle, and then he says I'm pretty just as I am, and I grin even more.

Mammy and John don't like me and Anna living so far away, and they keep trying to take us back to Scotland. We'd both like to go with them, but Fred and Rose don't want us to. One time, when Fred was back home, he started a fight with John, but John belted him and put him on the ground. Anna and me made a run for John's car and we almost got away, but some other men came along to help Fred, so Mammy and John had to leave without us. Mammy was crying. So was I, and so was Anna. I can't really understand why we can't go with them; Fred and Rosie don't treat us very nicely anymore, especially me.

Rosie sometimes seems to have the same idea as me. 'Why the hell didn't you just let them go?'

'No lanky bugger's taking my girls off me,' says Fred.

'The half-caste's not even yours, and you don't treat the other one like she's your daughter either.'

'What the hell do you mean? 'Course I do.'

'You *know* what I mean.'

He hesitates. 'I don't know what you're on about.'

'What Daddies do to their daughters. I've hardly seen you touch her.'

'I've told you before. She's still too young.'

'Well, it's time you started breaking her in, or no man will ever want her.'

After that, Fred starts putting his hand up Anna's dress, and Rose slaps her if she starts to cry. She slaps me too, of course. Just for the hell of it.

WE'VE MOVED to a basement flat in Gloucester and Fred's gone away again, and we are Rosie's prisoners. She's fitted bars along the side of our bunk beds, like a fence, so we can't get out unless she lets us.

'It's like a bloody cage,' I say to her. Big mistake. I'm put back in there for two days and nights with nothing to eat or drink. Anna can't sneak anything for me because Rose watches her all the time and controls her every movement. She has to clean the flat from top to bottom every day, and if Rose finds a speck of dust Anna gets a thrashing. I think Rose has got worse since she started getting a fat tummy and telling us she'll soon have a real daughter and she won't be bothering with us anymore. I'm looking forward to that, because Anna and me could manage just fine without the shouting and the beatings.

Fred's set up a video camera in Rose's bedroom, so that when men come to visit her, it all gets recorded and Fred will be able to watch it when he gets home. Rose can hardly waddle around now, but she still seems glad the men come. Some of them give her money. One gave Anna and me £1 between us once, but Rose saw it and took it out of Anna's hand. Sometimes we get lollies or sweets but we've learned to hide them till bedtime.

I don't answer Rosie back as much now. I get scared when she turns into a monster, and I know she's going to hurt me. She looks totally different. Like in that story; Jekyll and Hyde. Anna turns away but Rose tells her to watch what happens to wicked girls. Rosie's so big now though, that she has to stop and rest halfway through the beating.

I'M SEVEN NOW, AND ANNA'S SIX, and we're both big sisters. They've called the baby Heather. My teacher said it's a kind of purple plant that grows in Scotland, and I felt so homesick I burst out crying in class like a big baby and everybody laughed. My teacher didn't laugh. After school was finished she put her arm round me and asked if everything was okay; just like Miss Symonds once did.

'It's great,' I said, forcing a grin onto my face. 'Especially now I've got another little sister.' But it wasn't great. It was much, much worse.

I FEEL SORRY FOR ANNA, because now Fred's back, he does horrible things to her all the time. Sometimes he takes her into the bedroom and shuts the door, and sometimes I have to watch him put his hands all over her. And he makes her put her hands between his legs, and I feel sick. I can tell Anna feels sick too, and she cries afterwards. The trouble is; he's her real daddy, and she'll have to stay with him and Rose for ever. But I'm going to run away and find *my* real daddy. He won't do those things to me.

'COME ON, CHAR. Please. We'll get into such trouble.'

'Stop pulling my sleeve, Anna. You go if you want to. I'm staying a few more minutes.'

'My daddy could drive past at any minute. If he sees us, Char …'

I smile. 'That's why I'm here,' I say, trying to make sense of the bus timetable. 'So could mine.'

'But he's in Glasgow, Char.'

'Oh, people move all the time. He might've found out where I live and come to find me. Oh, here's one now.'

The bus lumbers up to the stop, and I push past the emerging passengers to get a look at the driver's face. He's a fat man with pale skin and no hair.

'On or off, mi duck? One way or another you need to get your foot off the step.'

'Sorry,' I mumble, as Anna touches my hand.

'Come on, Char. We can come again tomorrow if you like.'

She's a good sister. I'll miss her when I leave.

SOME DAYS, Rose keeps me off school and ties me to the bed. She puts a rag in my mouth and a plastic sheet underneath me to catch the blood and then she beats me. She spreads my legs apart and whips me with the buckle end.

'Cry, you little Paki.'

It's agony, but I won't cry. I hold the tears and the screams inside so she can't see or hear them. I've watched her beat Anna too, and when Anna cries Rose laughs and beats her harder.

One day, when Rose had me stood up on the stool with my hands tied behind my back, my friend Tina from the flat upstairs came to ask me to play.

'Does she do that a lot?' Tina asks me the next day.

I don't miss a beat. 'Oh no!'

'Because if she does I can tell my mum and she'll make her stop.'

'Don't be silly. She was just really mad yesterday. It's because my mam is coming for me soon, and Rose wants me to stay here with her.'

'So you'll be leaving Gloucester?'

'Yes, and I'll miss you, Tina.'

'Is Anna going too?'

'We don't know yet. She'd like to, but Fred's her real dad, so she might have to stay here.'

Tina sighs. 'But he's always away. Like now. Char, where does he go?'

I pull her round the corner behind the high wall. 'He's in prison,' I whisper. 'He's there a lot.'

'Has he killed somebody?'

I laugh. 'Tina, you're so funny! It's something about a car I think. Or maybe stealing. Anyway, I don't really care about Fred or Rose. I just hope Anna can come with me when I go.'

I DON'T HAVE TO RUN AWAY after all, because Mammy is coming for me today! I'm going to stay with her for a while. Rose says she doesn't want me anymore, so it might be for ever. And maybe I'll get to see my daddy! I hugged Anna as she set off for school this morning, not knowing when I'd see her again.

'Get away from that window! What are you doing?'

'I'm looking out for my mam, Rose.'

Rose narrows her eyes. 'I've told you to call *me* 'Mum'. Say it, or I won't let you go with her.'

'I don't want to, Rose,' I say for the hundredth time. 'Why do you keep telling me to?'

'Because it's me that's looked after you all this time. Where the hell's she been, that Rena, hey? Shacking up with that Scottish cowboy, leaving her kids with me.'

'I'm sorry, Rose. But you know she's always wanted to take Anna and me. It's you and Fred who've stopped her.'

She takes off her belt, but I don't care.

'Rose don't hit me. I'll tell my mammy.'

'Call me "Mum" and I won't belt you.'

'You'll soon be rid of me, so why are you bothering?'

'Call. Me. Mum.'

'No. I won't. You can do what you want but you're not my mum.' I turn back to the window but I feel her grab me by the collar and drag me backwards.

WHEN MAMMY AND JOHN come to the caravan later that day, Rose tells them I've run away. Mam screams at Rose that she shouldn't have kept hitting me and making me scared all the time.

Rose just laughs. 'She wasn't scared of anything, that one! She probably went off with some boys and that's the last we'll see of her.'

'She's eight years old!' shouts Mammy. 'Of course she hasn't gone off with any boys!'

'Well, I think we've seen the last of her anyway. And good riddance!'

'Please tell me where she's gone, Rose,' says Mammy. 'I'll just keep coming back until I find out.'

But Rose was right, of course. Neither my sister nor my mammy saw me ever again.

An Overview of Charmaine's Case

Charmaine Carol West
22.02.63 - June 1971
aged 8 years & 4 months
Gloucester, England

Most UK citizens will be aware of the two most notorious serial killers of the last millennium, Fred and Rose West. Many will recall horrific details of the torture of the helpless victims they hung upside down in their cellar, bound and gagged, enduring days of terror and pain as the married couple used specifically crafted tools to sexually torture them. Several will know that their crimes came to light when one of their younger children revealed the family 'joke' that their sister Heather (the baby born when Charmaine was seven), was buried under the patio. Digging up the pink and grey flagstones in 1994 proved this to be true, and along with other bodies, Charmaine's remains were eventually found, 23 years after her murder.

But how many remember Charmaine? The bright little girl from Glasgow who was caught up in the Wests' web many years earlier?

Charmaine Carol West was born in Coatbridge, Scotland on 22 February 1963, to Fred West's wife at the time, Rena Costello. Charmaine's father was said to have been a Pakistani bus driver, who Rena had met whilst working as a conductress. The relationship did not last; in fact Charmaine's father may never have known she existed, and Rena was still pregnant when she met Fred West. Although it is said that Rena was a good mother, she may have felt reluctant to proceed with the pregnancy, as Fred tried, without success, to abort the baby, using a homemade metal contraption he had especially made.

Rena had had a turbulent childhood, spending time at a girls' borstal; a school for troubled teenagers. Once her daughter was born, however, it is said that Rena's maternal instincts kicked in, and she became a protective mother, boasting that Charmaine's father was a wealthy businessman. To his credit, Fred West stood by his pregnant girlfriend, giving her mixed-race child his surname, and a year later, Rena gave birth to Fred's own child, Anna-Marie.

Rena Costello endeavoured to have her daughters living with her as much as she could. But Fred was often violent to Rena, and she would escape him by travelling around the UK, where she may have worked as a prostitute. At these times, Charmaine and Anna-Marie would be placed in care, or looked after by the succession of school-age children that Fred lured into the flat.

This pattern continued after Fred moved back, with the girls, to his home county of Gloucestershire, to a caravan on the Lakehouse Caravan Park at Stoke Orchard, where he soon took up with a pretty dark-haired teenager called Rosemary Letts, following their meeting at a bus-stop.

At first, 15 year old Rosie enjoyed mothering the little Scottish girls who lived with her new boyfriend, making them meals, sewing their clothes and teaching them how to knit. But as time passed, a mere child herself, and the product of a chaotic and incestuous family, Rose proved that she did not have the skills to cope with the normal behaviour of bright and lively children, and so turned to violence to try and keep them in line. Anna-Marie was pliable and obedient, but a year older, clever and strong willed, Charmaine was not.

It is not known whether Fred West played a part in Charmaine's murder. By the time she died in 1971, he had already killed at least two people, but it is generally believed that Rose West acted alone (and that Charmaine was her first victim), whilst Fred was in prison. But what made this evil couple capable of such atrocities?

§

Fred West's childhood was immersed in violence and sexual sadism. At the age of eight, he was taught by his father how to have sex with sheep, and how to rape little girls. In between beatings, his mother took him into her bed and molested him, over a period of many years. Whilst still a teenager, he got his 13 year old sister pregnant; incest being as natural to him as breathing. It is believed that the child was aborted, and when the girl would not name her brother in court, the case was dropped. Frederick Walter West had learnt the lesson that was to horrify the world 30 years later; that he could do whatever he wanted, and get away with it.

But it is Rosemary West who is widely acknowledged as the killer of her stepdaughter, Charmaine. And yet again, we see a childhood of unremitting abuse and incest.

§

Rosemary Letts was born in 1953, to an untreated schizophrenic father, and a mother whose depression was so severe that she underwent several courses of electro-convulsive-therapy, including throughout her pregnancy with Rosemary, the fifth of her seven children. The value of ECT is unclear; it is not known how it works nor how effective it is, nor whether in many cases it perhaps causes more harm than good. It is now used only rarely in the UK, and never on pregnant women.

In order to care for his sick wife, Rose's father, Bill Letts, was discharged from his career in the army on compassionate grounds. There is no evidence that the unfortunate woman's health improved on the return of her controlling husband, whose strict cleanliness regime she had to impose upon the children. For any perceived misdemeanour, Bill Letts would vent his rage upon his family, subjecting them to physical and psychological cruelty. Whilst his offspring strove to avoid his wrath and unpredictable moods, local children referred to him as 'schizo'. Furthermore, his wife's terror of her husband led her to treat the children in a similar way, so there was little respite from the fanatical cleanliness and fear. Daisy Letts, almost permanently pregnant, enduring a number of miscarriages as well as seven full-term pregnancies, found herself unable to leave her violent husband.

In common with many abused children, as a baby, Rosemary would bang her head against the sides of her cot, but as she grew older, in this atmosphere of rigid obedience and violence, young Rosemary Letts learned how to avoid her father's sadism.

Bill Letts attempted to groom his daughters into having sex with him, and Rose soon found that by becoming her father's plaything, she was able to evade his rage, and she quickly became his favoured child.

Bill Letts struggled to find permanent work, and moved his family from the village of Northam in Devon to the city of Plymouth, and from there, when Rosemary was eleven years old, to Bishop's Cleve, near Cheltenham in Gloucester.

Neighbours concerned about abuse alerted the authorities, but no charges were brought, nor support for the children given, reinforcing the fact that no outside agency was going to put an end to their suffering, and that they must learn to bear it until it was time to leave home. Bill Letts' incestuous relationship with Rose continued to grow, with the young girl learning to become immune to the abuse of her siblings that she witnessed, and revelling in the attention her father gave her. Around this time, the nurturing cuddles she gave her two younger brothers, with whom she shared a bedroom, developed into molesting them sexually, setting the precedent that continued with her own children; that she could control them however she chose, raising her self esteem.

By the time Rosemary was 15, Daisy Letts had succeeded in leaving her psychotic husband, eventually finding work on a farm with live-in accommodation for herself and the younger children. Initially, instead of moving in with her mother, Rose chose to sleep at the homes of the various older men she was having sex with, until the police noticed the behaviour of the teenage bakery worker, and cautioned her to return to her family. But to the astonishment of all who knew them, Rosemary chose to live with her father. Her acceptance, and possibly delight, in the bond she shared with this abusive man, paved the way for her relationship with the sex-crazed Fred West, who as we have seen, shared a similar past to her own.

It is doubtful that Rose had insight at the time about her abusive childhood, but many years later, she wrote from her prison cell: "My parents were sick people who should never have had children in the first place." And she goes on: "No one cared for us, EVER." The toxic blend of enforced sexuality and the desire to control and mother others began Rose's descent into the horrifically cruel matriarch she became.

Rose is the perfect example of someone who was unable to escape the chain of abuse, and a 'monster', who maimed and tortured for sheer pleasure, was created.

§

Rosemary Letts was working in a Cheltenham baker's shop when a scruffy man, 12 years her senior, began to take an interest in the pretty girl with the big brown eyes. And thus, the fates of several young women were sealed.

Fred charmed the 15-year-old with a lace dress and fur coat, but the clincher was his two little daughters. Rose 'loved' children, and made them a rag doll each, which she brought with her on her first visit to the caravan she soon made home.

At first, Rose was kind to the girls, accompanying Fred when he took them to pick flowers and run around in the surrounding fields, and she enjoyed the attention he gave her when they had sex as the children played close by. She was soon persuaded to give up her job in order to care for the girls full-time, and Fred was finding clients that Rose was happy to service with sex in the caravan. But her father found out and, somewhat ironically for a man who had been abusing his daughter for years, informed social services, and Rose was made to go to a children's home. Though she wrote loving letters whilst there, she found out that Fred's wife Rena had returned for a short while, and Rose became determined to make sure that she became the undisputed lover in Fred's life. She was back with Fred as soon as she could, and the family continued to live their unconventional life.

Rosemary West initially revelled in her role of mothering the two girls. Was the beautiful dark-haired teenager trying to right the wrongs of her own childhood by making dolls, cooking good meals and dressing Anna-Marie and Charmaine in clothes she had sewed herself? If she was, she was soon overwhelmed by the realities of bringing up children, discovering that they were not her playthings after all, and she lashed out in ways that sowed the seeds for her reign of terror over them, and the rest of the large family she later gave birth to. Handing over the discipline of the girls to his teenage partner, Fred told them "your mum does it because she loves you", while cautioning Rose not to 'hit the children where it shows'.

Following a couple of short term house moves, and after children's services had warned the Wests that if the girls were not going to be living in a stable home, they would not be returned from their most recent children's home to Fred's care, the family moved to a ground floor flat at 25 Midland Road, Gloucester.

Rose was often alone with the girls, with Fred busy working long hours or doing time in prison; his string of petty thefts having caught up with him. Rose relished the power she had over Charmaine and Anna-Marie, and her violent and cruel behaviour escalated, particularly when it came to Charmaine, who refused to bend to her will.

Whilst Anna-Marie was obedient and biddable, Charmaine was a bright and independent spirit, who refused the instruction to call Rose 'Mum'; her own mother still being in the picture, albeit sporadically.

Rena Costello tried many times to gain custody of her daughters, but Fred and Rose maintained their tight grip. Despite the girls' behaviour allegedly warranting frequent punishments, they refused to allow Rena to take them off their hands.

Infuriating Rose and denying her the control she craved, Charmaine refused to cry, inciting her stepmother to use increasingly sadistic methods to impose her will.

Charmaine was locked in the bedroom, strapped to the bed with her legs apart and her hands tied behind her back. She and Anna-Marie were gagged with cloth, and then with tape; a sinister precursor to the masks of tape bound round the heads of the Wests' later victims, with only a small hole to allow them to breathe.

When Rose gave birth to Fred's daughter, Heather (who they later murdered) and with her 'husband' (Fred was still legally married to Rena) frequently absent, the 16-year-old now had three girls to 'care' for.

Rose's abuse of the children continued, and when Fred was incarcerated in Leyhill open prison in early 1971, Rose took Charmaine to hospital with an injury to her ankle, probably caused by Rose stabbing her with a knife, and on at least one occasion, Anna-Marie came upon her sister spreadeagled on her bed, with a plastic sheet under her, clearly in a state of great distress.

During this time, Rose wrote the following words to Fred about her eight year old charge: 'Darling, about Char. I think she likes to be handled rough', thereby attempting to justify her own viciousness.

The precise date and manner of Charmaine's death remain a matter of speculation. One day, early in the summer of 1971, Rose kept Charmaine off school, for reasons not entirely clear, but one possibility is that there was an agreement to hand the child over to Rena that day. One of the theories around the eight-year-old's death is that Rose flew into one of her incandescent rages, and either strangled or stabbed Charmaine. Knowing Rose's fondness for bondage, another explanation is that she tied up and beat or otherwise abused the little girl, perhaps practising her 'torture skills' upon her, then realised that Charmaine would have to be disposed of so that she could not tell. She must have somehow managed to explain Charmaine's absence to Rena West if she then arrived to collect her daughter. Whatever the case, when Anna-Marie returned from school, her sister was gone. Rose told the school and anyone who asked, that Charmaine had gone to live with her mother, varying the location between London and Bristol.

(Later, Rena was also killed, presumably by Fred.)

Shirley Giles, who lived with her family in the flat above the Wests on Midland Road, testified at Rose West's trial. Her daughter, who had become Charmaine's best friend, had witnessed Rose forcing her friend to stand naked on a chair with her hands tied behind her back, whilst she beat the girl with a large wooden spoon. Shirley Giles also told the court that Charmaine had disappeared whilst Fred

West was in prison, corroborating the dental evidence which placed the child's date of death during this period.

It is believed that Rose kept Charmaine's body in the coal cellar, until her 'husband' was released from prison and was able to bury her in a hole outside the kitchen door. Her remains were moved three years later when Fred built a kitchen extension, and Charmaine was placed under the foundations.

§

Fred West hung himself whilst on remand for nine murders. Rose West was later convicted of ten murders and sentenced to 25 years in prison, increased in 1997 to a whole life tariff (meaning that she will die in prison). In the words of Leo Goatley, her solicitor from 1992 to 2004, Rosemary West spoke in a shrill, almost breathless voice, and often appeared like an ordinary housewife. But if asked questions she did not like, such as about her guilt of the numerous murders, her anger would explode, before subsiding into the silence of denial.

Charmaine's cremated remains were eventually placed in the same coffin as her mother Rena, who, in the short time between their two murders, had searched in vain for her missing daughter.

Rest Safely in Peace, Charmaine

Violence and Torture

Although Fred and Rose West may be grotesque and rare examples of extreme torturers, they are far from alone. Violence has always been part of life.

We need only look at atrocities perpetrated during the Atlantic slave trade, the Rwandan genocide, the Nazi concentration camps, etc, to see a person's capacity to hurt a fellow human being.

When someone has a human being more vulnerable than themselves completely within their power, their capacity for cruelty can prove to be horrifying.

§

To begin to understand how someone is capable of sadistic violence to a child, we need to visit the perpetrator's own childhood, where their environment contributes to the formation of their character, and we frequently find that they have grown up surrounded by those who use cruelty and violence as a response to even the mildest conflict.

We can never truly know the full picture of the murderers' experience of violence when they were children, and even within the same family, abuse is dealt out unequally, or perceived differently by those enduring it. But when it humiliates the child, and wounds their developing sense of self, they have to find coping behaviours.

By necessity, they may have to repress their true feelings of rage and frustration at having no control in the face of neglect or violence. As they mature, this frustration may be expressed inwardly, in the form of self harm, such as eating disorders, depression, etc. But some express these feelings outwardly, by dispensing violence to those over whom they eventually have power; their children.

Fascinating studies now show that when a child is constantly having to cope with or avoid their parents' abuse, the physiology of their brain is altered, switching off empathy (which is not needed) and switching on survival (which is needed). And their capacity for empathy may be permanently diminished.

If we overlook the effects of the perpetrators' own brutalised childhoods, we condemn generation after generation of innocent children to lives of horror.

NB – Those who were abused as children but do not continue the cycle of abuse may be rightly defensive when this aspect of abuse is discussed, so I wish to make the following points very clearly:

- **All abused children do not become abusers.**
- **Most abusive adults were abused as children.**

Two Weddings and a Funeral

'THE BLUE OR THE BLACK?' says Cheryle, twirling in front of the mirror.

'Hmm, I'd go for the black. Smart and classy.'

'Black it is then. Oh, I'm so excited, Syl.'

Sylvia nudges her friend. 'Can't say I'd noticed! But you deserve to have some fun.'

'I reckon I do! Haven't been out since Michael and me split.'

'Where's this Paul taking you?'

'That new Italian place, I think. But I'll be too nervous to eat!'

'Wha-at? If he's paying, make sure you eat as much as you can!'

Cheryle smiles at her reflection. 'Scrub up pretty well, don't I? Even after all the kids! And you and Wayne'll be alright?'

'Are you kidding me? Wayne's been looking forward to this all week! You know how he is with those kids.'

'Yeah, I guess so,' Cheryle laughs. 'Hey, look at me, going on a blind date; it's so weird!'

'Yeah, but you've spoken on the phone a few times, haven't you? And anyway, loads of people go on blind dates these days.'

Cheryle takes a deep breath. 'And you're sure Wayne's okay to walk me down there?'

''Course he is. Why wouldn't he be?'

'And if I ring, he'll come and pick me up straight away?'

'No hesitation.'

'Okay. Right, here I go.'

Wayne's waiting at the bottom of the stairs, with Brad wrapped round his legs and Daniel in his arms.

Little Cathy reaches up to give her mother a hug. 'Are you going all the way into Melbourne, Mammy?'

'No, sweetheart, just into town.'

'I hope he's nice, Mammy.'

'If he's not, I'll throw him into Albert Park lake!'

'Right, Cinderella,' says Wayne. 'Let's get you off to meet Prince Charming. See you in a few minutes, kids. You too, Syl.'

Wayne's back in no time.

'Well, what's he like?'

'I didn't actually *meet* him, Syl. What am I, her dad?'

'I know that. But did he look okay?'

'I think so. He's a pretty big guy. But then, Michael was big too.'

'Oh, I hope they have a great time. Although she's been doing really well on her own.'

'Yeah, I don't know why she joined that dating agency.'

'It was kind of on a whim, I reckon. Still, if he's right for her, that's great. If he's not, she can tell him to take a hike.'

Wayne shrugs. 'Right, let's get cracking and make these kids some supper. Daniel, what would you like to eat?'

'Chee bean!'

'Now that's a real shame,' says Wayne, winking at little Cathy. 'Because we're all out of cheese. And beans.'

Daniel toddles away and comes back with a block of Cheddar in his hand. 'Unky Way fib!' he says, placing the food at Wayne's feet.

'Nothing gets past you, mate,' says Wayne, and he grabs Daniel and tickles him until he's breathless with the giggles.

'Cheesy beans!' shouts Brad, and points to the kitchen.

'Well, come and give me a hand then, kids. Fancy meals take a lot of hard work!'

'Cartoons!' says Cathy, and Sylvia turns on the TV.

'Looks like we're all too busy to help, Wayne.'

Wayne rubs his eyes, and Daniel is beside him in an instant, giving him a hug.

'No cry, Unky Way.'

Wayne makes a sobbing sound.

'No, no cry. Unky Way no cry.'

Wayne gives a big roar and picks Daniel up and swings him round until he's laughing again.

'Chee bean!' says Daniel. 'Chee bean!'

'**HERE WE ARE AGAIN**,' says Wayne, as Cheryle opens the door.

'You don't mind, do you, guys? It's just Paul's got these tickets and ...'

'You know we love it, Chez. Don't even think about it. Go on, have a blast.'

'But it's the third night this week. You sure it's okay?'

''Course it is,' says Sylvia. 'Now, hurry up, or you'll miss the start.'

'See you later then,' says Cheryle, reaching for her jacket as Paul knocks at the door, and the three kids scurry into the corner of the room.

As Sylvia waves off Cheryle and her new man, Daniel clambers up onto Wayne's knee, and plants a kiss on his face.

'Miss me, Daniel?'

The little boy chuckles.

'You did, didn't you?' Wayne blows raspberries on his tummy, and Daniel squeals.

'Me too!' says Brad, and Wayne grabs him and does the same.

'Love you, Unky Way,' says Daniel. 'Love you, Auntie Way.'

Brad snorts. 'It's Auntie Sylvia.'

'Auntie Wiwia.'

Brad and Cathy laugh, and Daniel joins in.

'What about Mammy? Do you love Mammy?' asks Wayne.

'Love Mammy!' shouts Daniel. 'Love Daddy! Not love Paw.'

Wayne looks at Brad.

'He not love Paul. I not love Paul.'

'Well, that's okay. You don't know him yet. There's no rush.'

Sylvia comes through from the kitchen with lemonade. 'You're daft about those kids, aren't you?' says Sylvia.

'And you're not?'

'Well, maybe just a little bit.'

'You know, Sylv, I reckon we spend more time with the kids than Cheryle does since she met Paul.'

'She's in the honeymoon phase. Remember that, Wayne? It'll pass soon enough.'

'As long as she's happy, I guess. Right, where's that movie you wanted to watch, Brad?'

The kids are in bed and the babysitters are snoring on the sofa when Cheryle and Paul roll in.

'Hey, you guys!' Paul's voice matches his stature.

'Oh, hi Paul. The kids have gone to sleep, so ... y'know.'

Paul doesn't seem to catch on. 'Great concert, wasn't it, babes? Phew, what a night! Some tinnies, love.'

Cheryle hurries into the kitchen.

Wayne follows her. 'Brad's got kindy tomorrow, Chez. I think we should keep the noise down.'

Cheryle giggles. 'He is a bit loud, isn't he? Oh, but he's gorgeous. Here, grab a couple of these.'

'Let's have a toast,' says Paul, clinking his beer against Wayne's. 'Business is booming and I've met the best girl in the world. Life is good.'

'It's painting and decorating, isn't it, Paul?'

'Yeah, but I don't get my hands dirty very often these days.'

'He's the boss,' says Cheryle.

'Hey, Wayne' says Paul. 'Now I think about it, I think one of my guys says he knows you. Rich Trelawney.'

'Yeah, I know Rich. A real fair dinkum bloke.'

'If you say so! To me he's as much a bludger as the rest of them.'

Paul's voice seems to be getting even louder, and Wayne tries again. 'Hey, I wonder if we could keep it down a bit. For the kids.'

Paul stretches back and grins at Cheryle. 'They might as well get used to it, Wayne my friend. Because I'm moving my stuff in tomorrow.'

'HI WAYNE, THANKS for babysitting again tonight. The big man and me are off to the movies.'

'No worries, Chez. You know I can't resist the little fellas.'

'Well, they're in bed, so you might not see much of them.'

'Already? I was hoping to play with them, or at least grab a cuddle or two.'

'Don't disturb them, Wayne. They've been naughty today and Paul wants them to know there's consequences. He's upstairs with them now, making sure they know they'd better behave themselves.'

Right on cue, Wayne hears scuffling from the boys' bedroom.

'Get to sleep! Now! You'll be in for it when we get back if there's another peep out of you.' Paul stomps down the stairs. 'Those kids! Wayne, make sure you let me know if they move a muscle.'

'Oh, okay. You guys just go and have a good time.'

Wayne closes the door and breathes deeply. He walks through the lounge and kitchen, picking up a few empty cans and throwing them in the bin. There's something different about the place. He flops down onto the sofa and flicks on the TV but just can't settle. He soon jumps up again and makes his way to the youngest kids' bedroom. Like so many times before, Daniel looks straight at him as he stands in the doorway. Wayne waits for the usual smile, but the child just lies there, transfixed.

'Hey, Danny boy. Got a cuddle for your uncle Wayne?'

Daniel seems to stare right through him.

'Mammy and Paul have gone out, Daniel. I'm looking after you tonight.'

The smile isn't as bright as usual, but it's coming.

'Come on, son. Want to sit with Uncle Wayne and have a biscuit?'

Daniel's arms reach out and Wayne gathers him up. Brad is still gently snoring.

Back in the family room, Wayne looks around for Daniel's favourite wooden train. Then he realises; that's what's different. There isn't a toy in sight. 'Hey, Danny, where's the choo-choo? And Mr Popcorn?'

Daniel is staring at the door.

'Shall I go and find them? I won't be a minute.'

Daniel grabs his legs and starts to shake. 'No, Unky Way.'

'Okay, okay, little man. You come up here with me.' Wayne sits the little boy on his lap and strokes his arm. 'We'll just have some you and me time.'

Daniel tenses each time Wayne's hand passes over his elbow, and when he lifts the child's sleeve he sees why. A huge bruise, in various hues of purple and yellow, is spread over Daniel's arm. It's only then that Wayne notices the same on the side of his head.

'What happened, son? Did you fall?'

Daniel squeezes Wayne tightly round his waist and buries his face in his chest.

'Did someone hurt you? Was it Brad?'

'Hurt.'

Wayne sits up straighter and holds Daniel away from him so he can see his face. He's shocked to see the sadness in his eyes. 'Who, Daniel? Who hurt you?'

Daniel shakes his head and says nothing, reaching out for another hug. Wayne holds him gently, stroking his face, until the little boy nods off to sleep, and Wayne quietly carries him back to bed.

THE PAINTER cuts in expertly around the doorframe at Sylvia and Wayne's house.

'Wow, Rich. That's a real neat job you're doing.'

'Thanks, Sylvia. Nice to be appreciated for once.'

'Don't say that, Rich. Nobody could complain about your work!'

'Tell that to the boss, Syl. He's never satisfied.'

Wayne looks up from his paper. 'You work for Paul Aiton, don't you?'

'Sure do. But I've worked for better bosses in my time. You know him, Wayne?'

'Not really. We know Cheryle, his girlfriend. Sylvia's big mates with her.'

'I don't see much of her these days though,' says Sylvia.

'What do you make of Paul, then?' says Rich.

'I dunno. He's pretty loud, I guess. Chez seems happy enough though.'

'Ever seen him with the kids?'

'Come to think of it, no. Not lately. Why?'

'Oh, just some stuff I've heard him say at work.'

Wayne has long forgotten his newspaper. 'What sort of stuff?'

'Well, I probably shouldn't say. He is my boss and all.'

'Is he hurting those kids?'

Rich flushes. 'He brags about it. Tells the guys he can do whatever he wants to them.'

'What? What does he do?'

'No, I'd better not say. But he seems to like the power he has over them. If you're friends with Cheryle you might want to check it out.'

'I'm not sure we're welcome there any more,' says Sylvia. 'But I'll be sure to go tomorrow and find out what's going on.'

'Don't say I said anything though. Right, that's me done for tonight. I'll be back tomorrow to finish off.'

SYLVIA COLLARS RICH as soon as he arrives the next day. 'I've been to see Chez and the kids. And I spotted something when I was helping to change Daniel's nappy. Cheryle said she hadn't even noticed it. But it was a real big swelling.'

'Poor little mite. It ties in with what I've heard. Paul's been telling the fellas he gets the boys to do starries.'

'Star-jumps? They're only two and four years old! And he's making them do star-jumps?'

'Not exactly. He makes them stand as if they're gonna do a starry, then comes up behind and kicks 'em between the legs. Sends them flying through the air. To see how far he can make them go.'

'No! No, Cheryle would never stand for that. Paul's just a load of hot air. He's got to be.'

'There's other stuff too, Sylvia.'

'Oh God. What other stuff?'

'Me and a couple of the guys have reported him. Try not to worry, Syl. Leave it with Family Services. That's all we can do.'

'But what the hell has he done to them, Rich? I need to tell Cheryle. She needs to know.'

'I'm sorry. But your friend's gotta know already. For crying out loud; she lives with him!'

'I daren't tell Wayne. He loves those kids to bits.' She pauses. 'Listen Rich, I noticed Brad and Daniel both had bruises on their heads and faces. Cheryle said they fell when they were rough-housing. But, but can Paul be punching them?'

'I think so. I think he kinda throws them around the room. Just for the heck of it. And the fellas said, oh I can't say it.'

'Go on, Rich. Please.'

'They said he pushes the baby's face into his own shit.'

'What!'

'I know, I know. Look, it's in the hands of Family Services now.'

'I'd better ring them too.'

'Can't hurt, Sylvia. Hey listen, they'll soon get this sorted out. But I reckon your friend's gonna lose her kids if she stays with Aiton.'

'But she won't! She can't stay with him if that's what he's doing. Oh God, what the hell has Cheryle got herself into?'

WAYNE IS HARD AT WORK over the kitchen table, his tongue peeking out the side of his mouth.

'What on earth's that contraption?' laughs Sylvia.

When he looks up, his eyes are moist. 'It's for Daniel. If he wears this on his head, maybe it won't hurt so much when that bastard smashes him into the wall.'

Sylvia wraps her arms around his shoulders. 'Oh, Wayne. You're such a good man. But what's Paul gonna say? And Cheryle?'

'I don't know, love. But I have to do something. Those investigators are taking their time, and the boys are getting beat on every day.'

'I heard the police went there. And Brad showed them a stick that creep uses to hit them with. It can't be long now.'

'Pass me that velcro, Syl. I need to attach these two bits of rubber to it.'

'Like a boxer's head-guard.'

He nods. 'Let's hope it keeps him safe for now. When are you going round there again, honey?'

'You want me to take it?'

'If you don't mind. You can go when he's out at work.'

'Yeah, I guess I can. Hey, Wayne. I need to tell you something.'

'Uh-uh?'

'Chez and Paul. They're moving. They won't live so close any more. We won't be able to keep an eye on things.'

Wayne sighs. 'Well, let's hope the cavalry get there soon.'

PAUL AITON NAVIGATES his way through the pots and vases.

'G'day, mate. I'm looking for some flowers for me and my girl's six month anniversary.'

'No worries, mate.' The assistant holds up two bunches and points to a third. 'How about these? Or these?'

'I'll take the yellow ones. They're beauties. Hey, you've got a strange job for a bloke!'

'What? Oh, right. Yeah, I'm just helping my girlfriend out. I'm a sparky by trade.'

'Oh, that's handy. I need the wiring sorted on the house we've just moved into. How're you fixed for time?'

'Got plenty of it. Just tell me when and where and I'll be there. The name's Alan, by the way.'

'I'm Paul. If you can start tomorrow, we've got a deal.'

ALAN LOOKS UP at the drawn curtains at the upstairs windows as he waits on the doorstep of his new customers' house.

The woman who greets him is barely civil as she shows him inside. The peeling wallpaper and empty rooms aren't quite what he expected after meeting the smart and confident Mr Aiton.

'Hey, I thought Paul said he was in the decorating business!'

The woman scowls at him, so he shrugs and puts down his bag of tools and lets her show him where to start working.

She sits at the table flicking through a magazine.

'Kids out at kindy?' asks Alan.

'No, they're upstairs.'

He hides his surprise. It's a beautiful day out. Unseasonably warm for August in Melbourne. A day to make the most of letting the kids play outside. He straightens up. 'Where next, Mrs Aiton?'

'It's Ms Butcher. The boys' room. Upstairs and first left.'

Alan can hardly see his hand in front of him. He calls downstairs. 'Okay if I turn the main lights on?'

'Yeah, I guess.'

At first he thinks he's got the wrong room. There are no toddlers pushing toy trains around or cuddling teddy bears. He looks over at what could be two empty beds, blankets pulled up high. Then he makes out the kids' arms, rigid on top of the covers, and two pale faces, staring and silent. They hardly seem to be breathing.

'Hi there, little guys.'

If it were possible, they look even more terrified.

'Aren't you warm, fellas? I can pull one of your blankets away if you like.'

The older boy shrinks back, shaking his head.

'Okay, okay. I won't hurt you, mate. Look, I'll just get on with fixing these sockets so you can plug your games and the telly in again.' Alan scopes the room; there must some games or toys somewhere.

The smaller kid lifts his head off the dingy pillow and gives Alan a tentative smile. He looks about the same age as his own son, but so much thinner, and with bruising around his eyes.

'Hey there, little fella. How you doing down there?'

'Hurt,' he whispers.

'Where does it hurt, buddy?'

A movement in the doorway makes the child flop his head back onto the pillow and screw his eyes shut.

'Don't let these two disturb you, Alan.'

'Oh, they're not, Ms Butcher. But if you don't mind me asking, are they crook?'

'Not really. But they play so rough with each other they wind up hurting themselves. I sent them to bed to calm down a bit.' She turns to leave the room. 'Keep quiet, boys. Don't disturb the man.'

Alan touches the younger boy's hand. 'You okay, mate?'

'We're not supposed to talk to anyone,' whispers the older boy. 'Or we get the big stick.'

'Who gives you the big stick, son?'

'Not supposed to tell.' Brad shuts his eyes tightly and won't say another word.

Alan creeps down the stairs. 'Well, that's quite a bit of it done, Ms Butcher. I'll be back tomorrow to take a look at the kitchen.'

'Okay. See ya.'

THE NEXT DAY, Paul Aiton answers the electrician's knock. 'Hi, Alan. Come on in.' He's sweating as he props a stick against a chair. Cathy and her little brothers are lined up with their arms high in the air.

'Kids, eh?' says Aiton. 'They just won't do as they're told. I'm running out of ways to punish 'em! Hey, did I say you could put your arms down?'

The girl winces with the effort of raising her arms again.

Aiton shakes his head. 'Okay, that's enough for now. Come here and say "Hi" to Alan.'

The girl and the older boy step forward on shaky legs.

'Did you hear me, Daniel?'

'It's okay, Paul. Kids can be shy sometimes.'

'Oh, he's not shy. You're not shy, are you, Daniel?'

The boy is staring ahead, as if he can't hear or see anything.

'Daniel!'

He jerks his head up and stumbles towards them.

'Quickly, Daniel.'

'Look, it's okay, Paul. He doesn't look well.'

'No, he's fine. Get here, Daniel. Now!'

The boy almost trips over his own feet in an effort to drag his body forward.

Aiton grabs his t-shirt and pulls him the last few steps. 'Now, say "Hello" to the man.'

Daniel's eyes can't seem to focus. He's trembling uncontrollably as he mouths the word "Hello".

'I'm sorry,' says Alan, picking up his tools. 'I just remembered. I need to be somewhere. I'll see you later.'

'See what you've done, Daniel.' Aiton's nose is an inch from the little boy's. 'You've upset the man. Go and stand with your face to the wall until I'm ready to deal with you.'

'No, no, they haven't upset me. It's fine, really.'

'These kids are so friggin rude.' Aiton is almost shouting now. 'They'll know about it soon enough, though.'

'No, Paul. It's okay. They've done nothing wrong. Don't punish them. Please.' Alan turns to Cheryle. 'They've done nothing wrong.'

She looks away.

'I'll get off then,' says Alan, almost running out of the house.

He calls the police that same evening.

'**CHERYLE, LOVE.** Can you get that?'

'Paul, I think it's the cops again.'

'You'd better let 'em in, love. I'll just go out back for a smoke.'

'I'm sorry, Ms Butcher. But we've had reports about the kids again. This time we're gonna have to talk to them. Alone.'

'Sure, no problem. It's just the boys at home today. I'll bring them downstairs.'

Daniel and Brad shuffle into the room, and the cops ask their mother to leave.

The two little boys stand with their backs to the wall, and raise their arms in the air.

'No need for that, lads. Come and sit down,' says one of the officers.

'Can we?' says Brad.

The officer nods and pats the seat. 'Now, listen boys. We want you to tell us how you got these bruises, and you, little un, can you open your eyes wider for me?'

Daniel's eyes are so swollen, they're no more than slits.

'Attaboy,' says the cop. 'So kids, these marks and bruises; how d'ya get them?'

Brad reaches down the side of the sofa, trying to bring out a big stick.

The cop gives him a hand. 'This? They hit you with this?'

Brad nods.

'We'll take it away and have a real good look at it.'

'But, it's Paul's stick,' says Brad. 'He'll get mad again.'

'Don't worry, son. We'll take care of that. Listen, fellas, we're gonna get you down to the police station, and a nice doctor's gonna check you over.'

THE POLICE DOCTOR looks at his nurse for the hundredth time. 'I wish it didn't have to be like this, but what can I do?'

'But we can tell; surely we can tell. Please, Mike.' She gently smooths Daniel's hair back out of his eyes. 'You're a handsome little fella, aren't you?'

Daniel tries to smile.

She looks from Daniel to Brad, and back again. 'How could anyone hurt you? Either of you? It's beyond me.'

Daniel reaches for her hand, and she can't hold back the tears. 'Oh, baby.' She cradles him in her arms and feels him shaking.

'Stay with you.'

'Please, Mike. Please.'

'I'm sorry. I feel the same, but you know as well as I do that my hands are tied. There's no definite proof.'

'This system is fucked up, if you ask me. You know and I know what's going on in that home.'

The doctor shakes his head. 'Don't worry. I'll be very honest in my report. But at this stage, we have to wait.'

'But if we send them home … '

'Not go home,' whispers Daniel, holding onto the nurse. 'Stay with you.'

'See, Mike!'

'Please don't make this any harder than it already is. Their injuries *could* be accidental. I'm obliged to let them return home.' And he prises the little boy's fingers from around the nurse's hand.

PAUL LOOKS AT THE JUMBLE of toys and household items like a king surveying his kingdom, and rubs his hands together. 'We're gonna make some serious money today!'

A neighbour walks past with his dog. 'Great day for a garage sale, Paul!'

'Get yourself over here; you don't want miss all the bargains!'

The neighbour smiles and walks on.

Cheryle comes out with a tray of homemade lamingtons and fairy bread, and Paul pulls her into him and squeezes. 'Mmm, they look good, love. Just put them over there.'

The kids are nowhere to be seen.

'Daniel loves fairy bread. Maybe he could ... ' Cheryle stops when she sees the look on Paul's face. 'No, we'll leave him in bed. Anyway, he's still got that tummy-ache. But I'll have to pick Brad up from his grandma's soon.'

'Yeah, no worries. I'll go up and see how Daniel's doing in a bit. But right now ... let's get everything stickered up with prices and sell some of this junk!'

'What should we charge for these baby toys?'

'Oh, not too much, babes. We want to make sure we get rid of them.'

Cheryle picks up a cuddly clown. 'Mr Popcorn's Daniel's favourite, Paul. He might still want to play with it.'

'When? That kid's always too crook to play these days.'

Cheryle bites her tongue.

'Hey, get me another tinny, there's a good girl.'

'Thirsty work,' he smiles, as Cheryle hands the cold can to him, and he takes a long drink. 'Right, I'm going up to take a leak. Keep making the big bucks, girl!'

As he comes out of the bathroom, Paul can hear Daniel crying. He enters the darkened room and stands over the bed. 'Shut up, you snivelling little shit.'

Daniel tries desperately to choke back his tears. 'Tummy hurts.'

Paul grabs him by the back of his t-shirt and hauls him from the bed. Daniel screams. His stepfather slaps his face. 'I *told* you to quit that whining, boy. When did you start disobeying my orders?' He throws him down. 'If I come up again and hear you bawling, you're really in for it. Now shut up and get to sleep.'

He bounds out to the garage where Cheryle is putting stickers on old cooking utensils.

'Little fucker's whinging again, Chez,' he says. '*And* the fuckin' toilet's blocked for the tenth time this week.'

'Oh hell, how're we gonna manage?'

'Don't worry, love. I'll sort it.' His phone rings. 'Hey. Yeah, yeah, I know it's just ... Now you listen here, mate. That money ...' His voice gets louder. 'I've told you that, mate ...'

Cheryle touches his arm.

He brushes her off. 'For the last fuckin' time ...'

'Paul, I have to go and pick Brad up now, hun.'

'What? Oh yeah, hang on. Yeah, and you can fuck off as well, you lazy bludger.' He stabs the off button. 'Fuckin' tradesmen.'

'I've got to go and pick Brad up.'

'Sure, yeah. In a minute. Hey, what's that wooden spoon doing up for sale? Pass it over.'

'Aww, Paul. Don't hit him with that again. Remember I have to take him to the clinic. They'll look down there and wonder what's going on.'

He shakes his head. 'I told you, Chez. I'll discipline the boys. You've been doing it wrong for years. If he's gonna piss in the bath, he's gonna get whacked till he stops doing it.'

She passes him the spoon she'd hoped to get out of the house, and watches her boyfriend go back indoors. 'Don't be long, Paul. I really need to go and get Brad.'

Trembling and whimpering, Daniel hardly hears Paul come back into the bedroom.

'I fuckin' *told* you about that crying,' Paul roars, and punches Daniel once in the stomach. Hard.

Daniel screams. 'Mammy!'

'You think your mammy's gonna help you now, you little piece of crap?' Paul bashes Daniel again, waiting for his reaction in between each blow. 'You need to do as you're told, don't you, Danny boy? You need to know who's boss!' He pauses for breath. 'Well, let me tell you; it's me. I'm the boss of everybody and everything in this house.' Forcing the two-year-old to lie flat on his back,

Paul repeatedly punches him in the abdomen. 'Stop that fucking screaming,' he roars into Daniel's face.

When he finally tires, Paul goes back downstairs to his garage sale and his tinnies, and Cheryle can finally set off to collect Brad.

DANIEL LIES ALONE ON HIS BED.

He doesn't hear someone enter the room and start yelling. Doesn't feel himself gently picked up and placed in a vehicle. Doesn't see the bright lights of the Emergency Room.

Unable to open his eyes, Daniel does not see the look of horror on the faces of the nurses and doctors who surround his hospital bed. His consciousness fading, he doesn't feel the pain from his two broken collar bones and his crushed internal organs. He no longer cries with the pain in his penis and genitals, deformed by their battering with a wooden spoon. And his ruptured duodenum has ceased its agonising torture. His pain is over at last.

Because Daniel is dead.

An Overview of Daniel's Case

Daniel Phillip Valerio
21.04.88 - 08.09.90
aged 2 years & 5 months
Victoria, Australia

This adorable photograph was taken before Daniel's torture began; those taken in the last six months of his life show a very different little boy.

§

Daniel was the second son born to Michael Valerio and Cheryle Butcher in a town just south of Melbourne, Australia. Daniel's brother was two years his senior, and the boys also had an older sister and brother from their mother's previous relationship.

Cheryle separated from Michael and joined a local dating agency. She met the well-built painting and decorating foreman, Paul Aiton, in February 1990, and he moved into her home soon afterwards. And it was not long before Cheryle's two youngest children were showing signs of abuse. Concerned neighbours and teachers who called Child Protection Services reported the marked deterioration of the little boys, who had become 'ghostly pale', withdrawn and bruised. On several visits to the doctor, Cheryle Butcher claimed that Daniel was clumsy, and that his brother played roughly with him. On one occasion, the GP doubted these excuses and admitted Daniel to Frankston Hospital under the care of paediatrician Dr Edward Lowther. As with the majority of abused children who spend time away from their place of torture, Daniel thrived, eating well and enjoying the attention and cuddles. Sadly, he was thrust back into his nightmare after just five days.

Cheryle's friend Sylvia, along with her partner Wayne, were so concerned about Daniel that Wayne made an item of protective headgear for the toddler, in the style of a motorbike crash helmet. (Witnesses at the trial wept when shown the helmet; a heart-breaking symbol of Daniel's suffering.) I assume they were included in the many people who tried to get help for the boys. But of the 21 professionals who were alerted to the abuse, none made the successful intervention that could have saved Daniel.

Paul Aiton told his employees that he didn't like his new girlfriend's children, and bragged about throwing Daniel against a wall to watch him slide down, hitting the two-year-old on his penis with a wooden spoon, and pushing his face into his own faeces. (Aiton continued his boasting after Daniel died. And when Cheryle then accepted his marriage proposal – yeah, you read that right she married her son's murderer – Aiton told friends that despite being charged with her son's murder/manslaughter, he'd "married the kid's mother").

The 'starries' I outline in my story, and the enforced standing with arms in the air are all genuine punishments. Along with Daniel, his brother and sister, who were four and seven years old, were subjected to this and other forms of torture.

The occupant of the adjoining flat reported that the screaming she could hear above the sound of her television had her reaching for the car keys and driving around to escape the noise. She was lucky. The children were trapped.

Electrician Alan Brennan was one of the last people to witness the boys' treatment at home. Whilst working at the Aiton-Butcher residence, he was so distressed by the children's stillness as they lay on their beds, covered with bruises, with Daniel unable to fully open his swollen eyes, that he called the police. During one police visit, Daniel's brother told the officers about the beatings and showed them the stick that Aiton beat them with, and they confiscated it. The photos and doctor's report were not received by the relevant police department until after Daniel had died.

On the last day of Daniel's life, the family were holding a garage sale, but the little boy was in dreadful pain from his injuries, including two broken collar bones, and was not well enough to take part. He also had an undiagnosed condition of the bowel, which would have caused further agonising pain. Angered by the child's crying when he went upstairs, Aiton admitted that he lay Daniel on the bed and repeatedly punched him in the stomach.

At his death, Daniel was found to have 104 separate injuries, and is said to have weighed 10kg (22lbs) while his murderer was ten times his size at 105kg (230lbs). The average healthy weight for a child Daniel's age is 13.6 kg (30lbs). In addition to his broken collar bones and injuries to his face and jaw, Daniel's internal organs were crushed due to incessant beating, and his frail body was bruised from head to toe. A pint of blood was found in his abdomen and his duodenum was ruptured.

I have been unable to find any memorial place for Daniel other than the plaque beneath his grandmother's headstone in Rye Cemetery and Memorial Gardens, Mornington Peninsula, indicating that he is buried in her grave. The headstone reads 'In Loving Memory of Elaine Margaret, Beloved Wife Of ... Devoted Mother Of ... ' In stark contrast, there is no headstone for Daniel, and the plaque simply reads:

Daniel Phillip Valerio 21.4.88 to 8.9.90.

Aiton was divorced from Cheryle Butcher by the time he was put on trial. The individual who was later to become his second wife, saw fit to enter the court with a silver balloon emblazoned in red with the words 'I LOVE YOU'.

During Paul Aiton's trial, he testified that he was angry on the day of the murder due to the stress of the garage sale, the toilet being blocked, and a disagreement with a tradesman.

After two trials, Aiton was ultimately convicted of murder. His new wife, Linda, who was permitted four hour conjugal visits, said that her husband was rehabilitated, with the words, 'What happened to Paul all those years ago was then. It's not happening now'. I repeat; *What happened to Paul.*

Daniel's case is remembered for two major reasons. Firstly, it marked a change in the law that made reporting of suspected abuse mandatory for police, health and social workers. Secondly, as I've mentioned above, the boy's mother accepted a marriage proposal from his alleged murderer on the day after he'd killed her baby. Furthermore, *she went through with the wedding three months later, by which time Aiton had confessed* to the crime. She later divorced him.

§

Paul Aiton was released from prison after serving 19 years of his 22 year sentence. The Victoria (Australia) government minister for Crime Prevention, Andrew McIntosh opposed Aiton's release, and tried to reverse the decision of the parole board, but their word was final. Noel McNamara of the Crime Victims Support Association also opposed the board's decision, saying that crime victims should have a place on the parole board to prevent criminals being released early. David Provan, of the parole board, outlined restrictions to be placed on Aiton's behaviour, including abstaining from alcohol, no contact with people under the age of 18 without written permission, and staying away from Daniel's family.

I'll end Daniel's story with this from Barnados Australia:

"Every child has the right to be safe in their own home. Yet every day, right here in Australia, there are more than 145 substantiated reports of child abuse and neglect.

Every two weeks, one child dies as a direct result of assault. These children have been exposed to exceptionally difficult circumstances in their young lives – abuse, violence, poverty, drug and alcohol issues, mental illness, homelessness and disability. Many of them have never known what it's like to grow up in a safe, stable place with adults they can trust."

My thanks to Lianne for suggesting Daniel's story

Rest Safely in Peace, Daniel

The Spouse Who Stands By

Sixteen years after Aiton was imprisoned, Cheryle Butcher decided to break her silence and speak to reporters.

She does not express gratitude that she escaped criminal charges for neglecting to protect her children. Nor does she explain her blindness to her baby's terror, nor her reasons for marrying Daniel's murderer.

Butcher claims not to have noticed the swollen scrotum pointed out to her by her friend, and she overlooked his two broken collar bones in the last few days of Daniel's life. Over a period of several months, she gave a litany of excuses for her baby's very obvious injuries; he was 'clumsy and accident prone' and 'all small children bump into things' and he 'often fell from his stroller' and 'walked into the furniture'. She also claimed a blood disorder.

Additionally, Butcher complains that the government of the state of Victoria is failing to stop child abuse. Yet, if there is one person in a position to stop the torture of a child, it is surely the adult residing in that abusive home.

If she feels remorse, it is tainted by self-pity and the blaming of others. The italics in the following paragraphs are mine.

'He (Aiton) *apparently abused my older son*, and he even showed the police the stick he used to hit him. And still *the police were happy to leave him there.*'

Cheryle Butcher was present at this police visit, yet she distances herself from the situation. I appreciate that this may be a coping mechanism. She subsequently claims that she blames herself for Daniel's death and that she has nightmares about Daniel's murder. It would be strange if she did not.

According to the reporter, Butcher says that the 21 professionals involved with the family *had failed her.* That they continue to fail families, and children are still dying.

Amid the abdication of responsibility, Butcher does make some relevant points: 'Get some support systems, make counselling available, build refuges for women. If you think something is not right, check it out,' she says. 'Talk to your doctor, talk to a family member, talk to someone outside the house, and follow it through. If you have a gut feeling something is wrong, walk away and get help.'

She hopes that 'by speaking out, *others will be spared the pain and torment she now suffers.*' I understand that neglectful parents may feel terrible pain after their child is murdered. Perhaps it's a living hell. But surely their pain, even those who felt they had severely limited options at the time, is very much secondary to the pain of a child who was utterly powerless to escape.

What we learn from interviews with spouses can play a crucial part in saving children from torture and death. Perhaps they endured as neglectful or abusive a childhood as the victim and some perpetrators, and are poorly equipped to show true empathy and protect the child.

And Butcher's behaviour could be partially explained if she had also lived in fear of Paul Aiton; terrified that standing up to him would increase his wrath.

But if she were under Aiton's coercive control, would she not have been giddy with relief when he was taken into custody? If not, was she perhaps still under his spell in the early days? But to marry him, three months after Daniel's death? When he had confessed to the murder?

Ms Butcher says she now *draws strength from* her eldest child and her grandchildren, mentioning in particular a three year old child. I can only hope that this was taken slightly out of context, and that a grown woman, in her late forties, does not depend upon the support of a three-year-old, and that after all the years since her son's death, she *not only draws strength, for her own benefit, but gives it too.*

Regrettably, Butcher's interviewer does not report any mention of the pain and terror suffered by Daniel (and his brother). Only her own feelings, and how she was failed are discussed. Butcher and Aiton seem to fall into the category of child murderers who are incapable of seeing the child as a human being.

The Cage

(*The use of the word 'handicapped' in place of 'person with a disability' reflects the time and the age of the character, and not the author's pattern of speech.*)

FASTER. COME ON, GO FASTER. I'm nearly there. The sidewalk's filling up with daytime shoppers; seniors on their way to pick up their medication, mothers with kids in strollers planning to stock up on formula and diapers. A man in a Chevy honks at me as I step off the sidewalk to make way for a lady carrying four bulging grocery bags.

But I've made it. I've actually made it! Who'd have thought Walgreens would be my saviour!

I slow down and force myself to walk across the forecourt, then slip between the sliding doors. I need to look inconspicuous, although I guess my filthy jeans and T-shirt make me stand out from the crowd. I make myself browse up and down the aisles without grabbing a fitness bar or some glucose sweets from the shelves. If only I had a few cents in my pocket. But at least I can use the bathroom, put my head under the faucet to get a drink of water, and be on my way again.

I'm sure that guy is watching me. I turn and walk the other way.

'Excuse me, son.'

No, please no.

He touches my arm and I choke back my tears. 'Looks like you could use a cool drink. Ever tried the famous Walgreens malted?'

What! Why is he asking me that? All I can do is shake my head.

The man hands me the drink and I stutter my thanks.

'That's okay, son. You take care now.'

I gulp it down in the corner of the store, watching the doors.

'You okay there, Partner?'

Another Good Samaritan?

I nod.

'How about a couple of these?' He hands me something fruity and oaty.

'Thank you, Sir.'

What's going on? Why are people being so kind?

I look down at my clothes. They think I'm a hobo. A teenage (well, almost) hobo! Perhaps that's what I am now.

I lock the door behind me in the handicapped* bathroom. Oh, my face in the mirror! Like a hunted animal. I finish the malted then fill the cup with water from the faucet, and finish the first granola bar. I'll keep the other one for later. After washing my hands and face, I make my way up the side of the store. I'm gonna do it.

I'm really gonna do it. I'm going to get away. I'll find my real mom and even if she doesn't want me she might let me sleep on the floor a night or two until I figure out what to do next.

As soon as I get to the door, I'll start running again. I'm going to really stretch out my legs and enjoy every stride. I was good at track when I was in school. What a feeling! Running along without a care in the world. And if I can't find Mom, I'll sleep in doorways or in a park or on a beach, and I'll go to school and study hard. I'd like to be a writer. I could write about all of this.

'Christian!'

My blood freezes.

'What do you think you're doing? Worrying your dad and me!'

No! No, please no! Why didn't I get further out of the neighbourhood? Maybe there's a back door. I can still do this. I'm not going back. I can't. I just can't. I'm going to be free.

'Come on, Chris. We can talk it through.'

She's still got it. That look. There'll be no talking; that's for sure.

I flatten myself against the shelves. If only I could become invisible.

She's getting closer. There's only a senior couple between us. Can they help me?

'Sir, Ma'am. I …'

But she's there first. 'My son,' she says, almost apologetically. 'Always getting where he shouldn't be!'

'Help me,' I say. But they can't hear me.

'Shouldn't he be in school?'

'Absolutely,' says my stepmom. 'But can I get him to stay there?'

They shake their heads.

'Oh, he's not a bad kid really.'

That smile. That terrifying smile.

Shelves in front of me, a wall at my back. I lurch to the side. Straight into the malted guy.

'Hey, buddy. Take it easy now.'

'Thank goodness you've gotten hold of him, Sir,' says my stepmom. 'I've been worried sick. Come on, Chris. Let's get you home.'

AFTER THE BEATING, my stepmom visits with her friend in the trailer next door and I'm allowed into the living room with the rest of the kids. I ease myself down onto the floor.

Only my big sister Tanya smiles at me. 'You okay, bro?'

I nod. What can I say?

The Simpsons are on the TV and the younger ones are laughing. I try to join in but I know something terrible is going to happen, and if I didn't hurt so bad I might try and run again. But Dad would know. He's in his room as usual, on the computer. But he hears everything.

'Where's she gone?' I whisper to Tanya. 'She never goes out.'

Tanya looks embarrassed. 'Oh, a neighbour said she had something Kim wants.'

I let it go. What do I care what she's up to?

'I nearly made it, Tan. I was almost free.'

She squeezes my hand. 'I know, Chris. Just watch the TV and try not to think too much.'

Homer's up to his usual crazy stuff and Lisa's explaining what he should do. Tanya and the little kids laugh and I join in.

'Got it!' she yells, and stumbles in, carrying an old dog cage.

I feel sorry for Kaiser; that cage looks kinda small.

She snaps her fingers. It means I've gotta follow her. We go into Dad's room.

'Got it, Riley.'

He swivels his seat around. 'Hey, that looks great, Kim. Attagirl!' He kisses her.

Gross!

They place it on the floor beside Dad's computer.

'Fits real well in that space.'

I have to agree. But Dad doesn't usually want Kaiser under his feet all day. Although, I guess if he's in the cage, he won't mind it so much.

They open the little door.

'In,' says Kim.

I look around. Kaiser is nowhere to be seen.

'IN!'

IF IT WAS JUST the cage it might not be so bad.

But the next day, Dad throws out my mattress and props the bed-frame up against the wall. They tie me to the frame and I have to stay there all day. My arms and legs are stretched real taut and I beg them to untie me, and finally they do. But only so they can whip me and holler at me to quit complaining.

So this is my life now. If I'd have known, I'd have run right past Walgreens and into the trees at the end of the street and then kept running and running. But instead, I'm tied to the bed-frame all day, and forced into the dog cage all night. The only time they let me out is when I have to clean the trailer or I'm getting punished. They don't even let me use the bathroom. I hurt so much I want to cry all the time, but if they catch me they untie me and beat me. They make Tanya beat me too.

What did I do to make them hate me?

When I was in school, I remember Justin's dad used to bring him candy on his break from work, and I asked Justin if his dad ever beat him real hard. It was like I just spoke Martian. I think I knew right then that my parents weren't the same as everyone else's. Justin kept out of my way a little after that and I was on my own at recess. Sure, I was lonely but I just used to run around, and sometimes the teachers would talk to me, so it was okay, I guess.

When I got tired of running, I used to sit down on the patch of grass at the edge of the schoolyard. One day, I felt something tickle my hand, and when I looked round there was nothing there. I thought it was just a few blades of grasss blowing a little, but it kept on happening, and on the 4th day I caught sight of it; a deer mouse! He was so cute, and he became my friend. I used to talk to him and get him black raspberries to eat. I even got to stroke him a time or two. Just before they took me out of school, he'd started waiting for me on our little patch.

That seems so long ago now.

'GET OUT, BOY. Hurry up!'

I was dozing, my face pressed against the bars of the cage, and when she yanks the door open I topple half way out.

She hands me a blue cloth. 'Wipe your hands and face. Now, come on.' She pushes me into the living room, and I blink in the unfamiliar light. 'He's been reading up on Geography,' says my stepmom to a woman sitting in the corner of the room. 'He has a quiet space we set aside for him to study.'

'That's good,' says the visitor, and she puts a mark on the paper in front of her. A checklist. 'What textbook is he using?'

My stepmom turns to my sister. 'Tanya, go and get Chris's Geography book. It'll be near your father's desk.'

Luckily for Kim, Dad keeps an atlas on a bookshelf full of video games.

'That's it, Tanya. Thank you. Chris hopes to travel one day, don't you son?'

'Yes, Mom.'

Miss Walker turns to me. 'How about English composition? Your teachers tell me you used to love to write.'

Kim steps in. 'We just ran out of paper, didn't we, Chris?' She ruffles my hair. 'He's been writing so much.'

'No problem. Here, take this.' Miss Walker passes me a notepad and when I flip the cover the pages are pure white. 'You can write as many stories as you like now. How about you write something for me now, Chris? Then I'll put it in your file.'

I can write what I want? And I have a file? 'So, it's just for you, Ma'am?'

'She said so, didn't she?' says Kim. 'Come and sit up at the table.'

'What should I write about?'

'Anything you like!'

My stepmom and Miss Walker chat about dogs and the weather, and I sit in front of the empty page.

It feels good to hold the pencil, and at first I doodle in the corners; lines and circles and squares. But before I know it, I'm writing about my life since that day in Walgreens, and I'm choking back the tears. I've just written how I wish that someone would check on me (I mean *really* check), when Miss Walker collects the piece of paper and scans the beginning where I've written that my sister is good to me, and the other kids like watching cartoons. She pops it into a brown file. 'Thank you, Chris. That's great. Ms Kubina, I'll leave this pad of paper with you so that Christian can continue his writing. It's really good for him.'

'Oh yes, we know,' says Kim. 'He loves writing, don't you, Chris?'

'Yes, Mom.'

'Homeschool is really working well for us, Miss Walker. We'll be able to carry on, won't we?'

'Oh, I don't see why not! Right, I'd better be going. Bye-bye, everyone. See you in a few months.'

'We'll look forward to it,' says my stepmother.

'HEY, TANYA.'

'Hey, Christian.'

It's a long time since Miss Walker came. I wish she'd come back like she said she would.

'You know what you've gotta do?'

Tanya touches my hand. 'I know, Chris. I've done it before.'

'I don't remember. I'm forgetting a heap of stuff, Tan.'

'I guess anyone would. Try not to worry, bro. You're doing good.'

'So, noodles again?'

'Yeah, noodles again, bro.'

'Anything to drink?'

'Sorry Chris, not today. Her orders.'

My skinny 15 year old sister helps me up into a sitting position.

'I'm so thirsty.'

'I know. I'm sorry.' She starts to hand me the spoon.

I hold up my swollen hands, trying to grin.

'Guess I'll have to feed you.'

'Sorry, sis.'

She manages to force a few spoonfuls down before the sticky mess starts to choke me. 'You have to eat it, Chris. You know that.'

'It's just so thick, Tanya. It sticks halfway down.'

'Please try, bro. She's just out back. Waiting for the dish.'

'Can't you help me, Tan?'

She eats a couple of spoonfuls then tries me again. It won't go down. The last mouthful is lodged in my throat, and I cough. If I don't eat it, Dad will hurt me. More than usual, I mean.

'Under the bed? Or behind the closet?' I croak.

'I'll have a look.' She crouches down, then stuffs the remaining stodge in with the rest of my leftovers. She shows me the empty dish. 'Pretty good, bro. Should be okay.'

'Thanks, sis. If only I could have a drink.'

'I'm sorry.' She secures me back onto the upright bed-frame. 'See you later then.'

'Yeah, okay. See you later.'

I try to pass the time by remembering good things that have happened, like a film I've watched or a book I've read. I used to be able to name a book for almost every letter of the alphabet. Around The World In 80 Days, Black Beauty, Charlie and the Chocolate Factory, and … and … Oh, I wish I could have a book to read. I wouldn't mind what it was. Just something to escape into.

Apart from the boredom and the pain, loneliness is one of the hardest things. None of the little kids come in to see me, and Tanya's only supposed to come when she's feeding or punishing me. But I can always hear the hum of the TV, and sometimes I hear them all laughing or arguing. I miss all that stuff. Why does no one like me?

My dad told them I did a bad thing and it made them scared of me, I think.

TANYA COMES BACK at seven in the evening.

'Seems quiet out there.'

'Yeah, Stepmom-from-hell's watching TV with the kids, and Dad's out.'

I nod.

'But I've still got to, y'know.'

'I know, Tanya. What is it tonight?'

'The bath.'

'Not freezing, sis. Please.'

'I'll try. But she'll hear the hot water if I run it.'

'Okay. Maybe not so much ice then, huh? It's just, I don't feel so good.'

'I've gotta go run the bath, Chris.'

At least I'll be able to drink some of the bath water. Not too much though, or I'll get beaten for wetting myself.

Still dripping, I hobble back to our father's bedroom, while she mops up the bathroom. I'm so bent over now I scarcely have to crouch to fit into my sleeping quarters. She strokes my fingers as she slots the last padlock into place.

'Okay, little bro?'

'Okay, big sis. Goodnight.'

TANYA'S UP EARLY to change my diaper, creeping up to the cage so she doesn't disturb our father. 'Oh God, Chris,' she mutters. She knows I can't help it, but it gets to her; all this piss and shit, and me 13 years old.

My head is lolling, too dazed to answer. She can tell Dad's been at me during the night.

A couple of hours later, my screaming tells Tanya our father's up and it's time to make his breakfast. I can still hear them as he staggers through to the kitchen, hairy belly straining under the greying vest.

'Hope you're not being too fucking soft on him, lady.'

No hesitation. 'No Dad, of course not. I hate him just as much as you do. As much as we all do.'

'Yeah, well don't think we aren't watching you. Don't think that for a moment.'

'I know that, Dad. But there's nothing to worry about.'

I hear him slap her. 'Just don't forget, that's all.' He comes back into his room with his bowl of oatmeal, and sits down at the computer beside my cage.

'Hey Christian, you piece of shit. Daddy's staying home today. I'm gonna be right here the whole time.' He reaches down and pushes a spoonful of the cereal through the bars of the cage.

'I can't … can I have a drink of water first, please Dad?'

'You don't get to ask for nothing, you dirty dog. Eat it.' He's rocking the cage with his foot, making me feel sick.

The claggy mixture stays in my mouth, though I try with all my might to swallow it down.

Dad reaches out for the metal pole. 'You'd better do as I say, boy. Now eat it!'

I give a huge gulp, and immediately vomit it up again.

'You ungrateful bastard! We give you good food and this is what you do!'

After he beats me, he puts me back in the cage, then jabs his penknife through the bars. 'Don't you dare fall asleep. I want you ready when I'm ready. Do you hear me, son?'

'Yes, Dad.'

'Did you enjoy hurting those kids, Christian? Huh? Playing the hump game?' He shakes his head. 'Disgusting'

In the afternoon, when Kim and the kids are out, Dad drags me out of the cage and tells me to clean the trailer. He laughs when I can hardly lift the bucket, and then goes back into his room.

I used to like being free for a couple of hours; stretching my arms and legs. But now my limbs are so stiff it takes me ages to get moving, and I know Dad will be timing me. My fingers can't grip the brush either, so I'll be whipped for not doing it right. And I'm so tired. I know I shouldn't be, because I hardly do anything all day, but I feel exhausted all the time.

TANYA HAS CREPT IN while everyone else is glued to the TV.

'I wonder what our real Mom's doing now,' I say. 'You could go see if you can find her, Tan.'

'I wish you'd stop saying stuff like that, Chris. How could I possibly find her? Anyway, she wasn't much of a mother; she didn't want us.'

'We don't know that for sure, sis. Maybe she tried her best to keep us. Maybe she'd want us now.'

'I don't think so, bro. Don't forget, it wasn't all rosy back there either.'

'Better than this though. For me anyways.'

'Well yeah, I guess.'

'And the boyfriend might've gone by now.'

'I hope so. For the sake of the other kids,' says Tanya.

'And hey, now that we're older, we wouldn't be so much hard work.'

'Don't you think she would've come looking for us if she'd wanted us?'

I lean back onto the frame, and look up at the flaking paint on the ceiling. 'I'd even still sleep in a cage if Mom wanted me to. But a bigger one; one that I could lie down in.'

'Aww, Chris.' She doesn't cry much about me any more. But I know it sometimes gets to her.

'Don't cry, Tan. Hey, I bet she'd even let you go to school.'

'I'm getting too old for that. But maybe she'd let you go!'

'Me? Yeah, right!' It hurts me to laugh, but it's worth it.

'You were a good student, Chris. Better than me. I can't understand why the teachers or the welfare people haven't been lately to see how your homeschooling's coming along.' She laughs and shakes head. 'Homeschool!'

'I don't think they'll come now. Hey, I might ask Dad for another pencil and some more paper tomorrow. I still like writing.'

Tanya raises her eyebrows and gives a sideways look at my swollen, purple hands. 'Oh yeah, sure. You write it all down, with those fat fingers!' she says. 'Hey, Chris.'

'Yeah?'

'Did you do it?'

'Do what?'

'What Dad says you did. Y'know, touch that little kid.'

'No, Tanya! I've told you that.'

'I don't know who to believe.'

I give her a rueful grin and my version of a shrug. 'I'm not lying, Tanya. I'd never lie to you.'

'Well, I'd better get back before I'm missed.'

She's startled by movement in the doorway behind her, and sighs with relief that it's just our step-sister. 'Oh, hey Donna.'

'What are you doing in here, Tanya? Dad'll kill you.'

'I was just going. They didn't notice I wasn't there, did they?'

'No. No, I guess you're fine. One good thing with there being so many of us kids. But Mom says it's time for you to start.'

'Already? Okay, what is it tonight?' says Tanya.

'Whipping,' says our step-sister. 'See you later, Tan.'

Tanya turns back to me. 'I'm sorry, Chris.'

I take a deep breath. 'It's not your fault.'

'Well, I'd better get on with it. And scream really loud. They said I didn't hurt you enough last time.'

'Sometimes I'm just too tired to scream.'

'Try, Chris. Please.'

After the tenth stroke, our stepmother ambles through from the lounge, and throws a sock and a roll of duct tape at Tanya.

'Put a sock in it.' She laughs at her own joke as my sister picks up the sock, still damp and stinking from my father's foot, and rams it into my mouth. I retch as she sticks the tape over it.

My face is turned to the side, the metal springs tearing into my cheek, and I fight for breath.

The big woman crosses her arms. 'Well, carry on then.'

Tanya lets the belt fly onto my back and split my partially healed skin open again. Our stepmother nods her approval.

'This is what you get for molesting kids!' she yells at me.

I've heard that a thousand times. But I never molested anybody.

'Dirty, disgusting boy. Only fit for a cage like the dog that you are.' When she hears the end of the commercial break, she trudges back to her soap opera.

'I'll just do one more and then stop,' whispers Tanya, checking that none of the other kids are lurking around. She stays in position, belt in hand, for another five minutes.

'That'll do, Tanya,' yells our stepmother from the living room, and my sister's legs buckle. She rips off the tape and yanks out the sock. I gasp and gulp in the air.

'Leave the gag on though.'

'No, Tanya. Please don't. I can't stand it.'

I can see Tanya drifting away. Like she always does when it feels really bad. She's told me she goes to a place where I'm still part of the family, having fun with the rest of the kids, riding my bike, going to school. Where she's allowed to love me like other big sisters love their little brothers. Where she doesn't have to torture me.

She lets herself drift back to reality when I'm back in the dog cage, wearing nothing but a diaper, my limbs purple and swollen from being tied spread-eagled to the bed-frame for hour upon hour.

I **WONDER IF ANYONE** will ever read the things I've written. I used to write down that I wished someone would come and rescue me. But nobody came, and that's a long time ago now. Aren't they supposed to check on us homeschooled kids? I've tried to keep my spirits up, but I can't do it anymore.

That's why I've decided to try and end it. No one will miss me apart from Tanya. Maybe Donna. Dad and Kim won't miss me. They've told me often enough that I'm a waste of space. It worries me that they might start picking on one of the younger ones when I'm no longer around. That's what's stopped me from trying to end it before now. But I can't carry on any longer. Years and years more of this. I'll have to find a way to get Tanya to help me.

'**TANYA, WHAT'S THE CAGE FOR?** I mean, why am I kept in it?'

'Oh, Chris.'

'No, tell me, sis. I'm trying to make sense of things. I sometimes think I'm going mad.'

'It was after that time you ran away. Remember, Kim found you in Walgreens.'

'Oh, yes I remember. I was nearly free. I could've gotten far away from here.'

'Oh Chris, don't cry.'

I gulp down my tears. 'But the cage?'

'Yeah, it was after that. Mom bought it off a neighbour who didn't need it any more. Put you in it so you couldn't get away again.' She reaches out her arms. She risks holding me, just this once. 'Maybe I'll ask them if you can come into the living room and we'll watch Toy Story together. Remember that, Chris?'

'Woody and Buzz; 'course I do!'

She squeezes me, then has to let me go.

'And another thing, who's that little guy who comes to see me?'

'What little guy? It's always just me, or Kim, or Dad.'

'Don't mess with me, sis. The hobgoblin.'

'The what?'

'You know; like in that Spider-Man comic book I once had.'

'You really say some weird things, Chris!'

'I'm scared of him, Tan. Please don't let him come again.'

'O-kay, I won't.'

'He brings me soda and then puts pepper in it.'

'I think maybe you dream him up, Christian.'

'No, I don't. He comes here when no one's looking.'

'What's that crazy kid talking about now?' The stepmother is standing in the doorway, cackling. 'You'd better eat your slop, kid. Else you'll go nuts.' She slopes back off again.

'I feel scared when it gets dark, Tanya.'

'I thought you used to like the dark. You said nobody could find you.'

'But they can now. They can find me any time and any place.'

'Who, Chris? Do you mean Kim? Or Dad?'

I laugh. 'Well, yeah them too, I guess. But I mean *him*. You know, the hobgoblin.'

'But there isn't … oh never mind, bro. Just try and get some sleep before you make me as crazy as you.'

'Don't go yet, sis.'

'Go, how can I go? You're not in the cage yet, and I have to, you know, put the gag on.'

'I know. But I mean, I want to ask you something else.'

'What is it? Hurry up, Chris.'

'I'm ready to go, Tanya.'

She smiles. 'Where to? Disneyland? Remember, I said I'd take you there one day.'

'No, it's not that. I'm ready to go. To die, I mean. I was thinking; you could strangle me. Or drown me in the bath. Yeah, drown me, Tanya. Please. No one would know you did it on purpose.'

'Chris! You're out of your mind! I'm not doing that. No way!'

'Please, I'm begging you. Or just let me sink under the water. I can do it myself. It'd be so easy.'

'No, Chris. Don't ask me that again.'

'But I can't stand it anymore, I just can't.'

I scream with frustration and fight against her as she puts the sock in my mouth. But I'm no match for her.

IT'S BEEN DARK FOR HOURS. Dad and Kim must be out because I can hear the kids running around and jumping on the furniture. I've stopped wishing I could join in. All I can think about is ending my pain. No one is going to save me; I know that now. If only I could hold my breath; but instead it insists on rising and falling through the gag. I try to shift my position in the cage to relieve some of the weight where the bars dig into my flesh and make weeping sores, but I haven't got the strength. Why won't my body give up? Why won't my heart just stop beating? My life is hell and I want out. There's no hope, none at all. If only Tanya had agreed to help me.

The hobgoblin's been to see me and this time he talked with me real nice. And I think he's come up with the answer. I just need to stop eating. He said that's how I'm gonna get out. I told him I've tried that before but Dad forces me to eat, and hurts me real bad if I leave anything in the dish. I explained that's why Tanya eats some of my food, and hides the rest in the closet. But the hobgoblin said I shouldn't worry any more, because he'd eat it all for me, so my dad won't know.

He's here now and settling down to the bowl of noodles, so I let myself relax and doze for a few minutes. I feel sure I'm smiling in my dreams.

When I wake up, he's gone. Out of the corner of my eye I make out a familiar shape in the middle of the floor. My food bowl! And it's still almost full! How could he have done this to me? He promised! I have to think what to do. I don't think there's any way I can reach it, but I've got to try anyway. I know my dad will give me hell if he sees that bowl. And I just can't face another beating. Or another day of crouching in this cage as Dad sits beside me on his computer, yelling at me or rocking the cage till I'm sick.

Please let me die.

I hope God and Heaven are real, because I just want to go there. Nobody here cares about me, but maybe God will love me.

Then I hear the thud of his footsteps coming down the hall. 'Daddy's here, Christian.'

An Overview of Christian's Case

Christian Milton Choate
27.12.95 - 02.04.09
aged 13 years & 3 months
Gary, Indiana

One night in spring 2009, Christian Choate, a 13 year old boy from Gary, Indiana, was unable to chew or swallow the food his father demanded that he eat. Riley Choate flew into a rage and beat the boy mercilessly before throwing him back into the cage he was made to live in. That night, the boy died alone in the cage. The cause of death was blunt force trauma, internal bleeding, and skull fracture.

Christian's early life was clouded by abuse and neglect, and after her boyfriend was accused of molesting the two children, their birth mother lost custody of Christian and his sister. However, he had attended school up to at least second grade, and aunts on his mother's side have described him as a typical little boy who loved hot wheels, action figures, Pokemon, and the movie Toy Story.

Following the abuse allegations, the siblings were sent to live with their father and his wife, Kimberly Kubina, and their large brood of children, despite Riley Choate himself also having been accused of abusing his son, along with two of his nieces who lived in the family home. (After being removed to a place of safety for several months, the two girls who had been 'inappropriately disciplined' were returned to their uncle's 'care'.)

Both his father and his stepmother abused Christian from the moment he moved into the single width trailer, which housed the family of two adults and ten children. He was made to eat leftover food, and was beaten with fists and a metal pole.

In 2007, Choate Sr and Kubina stated that they were to begin homeschooling Christian. In reality, because of the lack of reporting required from homeschooling families, this gave them the opportunity to escalate their existing abuse of Christian, unobserved by the authorities. He must, however, have been seen by the Department of Children's Services at some point, because their records show evidence of Christian writing that he wondered when 'someone, anyone, was going to check on him'.

Once, the desperate boy managed to run away and get to a nearby Walgreens, but his stepmother found him there, and she subsequently bought the three foot high dog cage to keep him in. His father claimed that Christian had molested one of the younger children, (Riley Choate described it as 'playing the hump game') and therefore should be kept in a cage like a dog. No reports of this alleged abuse were ever filed. Sometimes the boy was let out of the cage and made to clean the family home, or was tied to an upright bed-frame to be whipped and punched. His sister was also made to punish her brother, under the threat of receiving the same treatment herself.

Although on at least one occasion, Christian told a medical practitioner that he was made to sleep in the cage, it went uninvestigated, and he was treated for anxiety and depression. When given pen and paper, Christian at first used to write that he just wanted his family to love him, but √as the months went on, he wrote that he wanted to die. When he tried to refuse food and then subsequently vomited the small amount he was forced to eat (which kept him alive but starving), he was brutally beaten.

The cage was kept beside Riley Choate's computer, where he often spent time playing video games, so there was little chance of respite for his son. Unsurprisingly, Christian's mind began to fail, and towards the end, in addition to the physical torment he was forced to endure, he suffered from hallucinations.

After beating him to death, Christian's father buried his body in a shallow grave, under a layer of concrete in a shed on the family property. Riley Choate stated that no one would miss Christian. Tragically, in a way, he was right. The family moved away, and the boy's death went undetected for more than two years.

Christian's sister, who had been forced to punish her brother, traced their birth mother and found the courage to tell her about his fate, and the truth about Christian's dreadful life was revealed. In due course, his father and stepmother were put on trial. One of the Deputy Prosecutors on the case, Michael Woods, said: 'Christian Choate sat in that cage, losing his mind, losing his strength and probably his humanity.'

In 2011, Christian's stepmother Kimberly Kubina divorced Riley Choate and co-operated in his prosecution, securing herself an early release, following her conviction for felony neglect. Riley Choate agreed to a deal to avoid a trial by jury and a possible murder conviction by also pleading guilty to felony neglect. In early 2013, he was sentenced to 80 years. Sheriff John Buncich, who handed down the sentences, described Choate as an animal.

In an interview with CBS2 investigative journalist, Brad Edwards, Riley Choate said, 'Did I fail him? Yes, I failed him'. And he then said these immortal words, '*I think I'm the only one who loved him.*'

Christian's torture and murder is one of several examples of abusing parents removing their victim from school in order to continue and escalate their actions away from prying eyes. In Volume 1, I tell the story of Jeanette Maples who was 'homeschooled' by her mother in the months before her death. Such parents have nothing in common with responsible caregivers who, along with the child, make the decision to offer the child a healthy, educational environment in the family home. But all homeschool situations should be regulated so that the positive practices can continue, and the abusive ones exposed. This regulation need not be a forensic examination of parents' every move; just basic safeguards to protect vulnerable children.

Rest Safely in Peace, Christian

The Child As A Lesser Being

Christian's father and stepmother viewed the little boy as so far beneath their level, that they kept him in a dog cage. They are not alone; thousands of abusers simply don't see the child as a human being, equal to themselves.

One child murderer viewed his victim as a novelty act, fascinated by her capacity to endure pain, and saying in court, 'You could beat her and she wouldn't cry ... she could take the beatings and the pain like anything'. And yet that child was a fellow human being, who had simply become too hopeless and exhausted to cry.

The law seems to support the notion that children are not equal to adults. In some US states, someone who intentionally kills another with a single gunshot to the head, their victim dying instantly, risks a conviction for first degree murder, with a sentence of life in prison or the death penalty.

In contrast, someone who subjects their child victim to a catalogue of deliberate cruelty spanning months or years, is often charged with murder in the second degree, because they did not set out to intentionally kill the child.

No matter that the victim suffered so much for so long. No matter that the obvious outcome could only be death, the perpetrator can stick to their story that they didn't actively intend to kill.

In the UK, murder and the lesser crime of manslaughter work in a similar way. One step towards redressing this imbalance is surely to ensure that sentences for torture (particularly when it leads to death) are overhauled and made to fit the severity of the crime, and the sentence for the murder of a child is at least equal to that of an adult; thereby dispelling the idea that the child is of lesser importance.

Following the efforts of Tony Hudgell (whose birth parents severely abused him, inflicting life-changing injuries), his adoptive parents, and his supporters, Tony's Law, implemented in England and Wales in November 2021, increases the maximum sentence possible for causing or allowing the death of a child, from 14 years to life. The maximum sentence for serious harm to a child is to be increased from 10 years to 14 years. Whilst prevention is the greatest gift we can give a vulnerable child, perhaps we can hope that these harsher sentences will act as a stronger deterrent against these crimes.

JESSICA JACKSON

Neighbours

THE BELL TINKLES and she glides through the beaded curtain and into the shop. 'Oh, hello again. You're my best customer this week! Is there something else you've forgotten?' She's flushed, as if she's been called away from the stove.

'Uhm, kind of.' I pretend to scour the shelves, before turning back to her. 'I keep forgetting to ask your name.'

She tosses back her hair and laughs. 'Oh, it's Samina.'

'Nice to meet you properly, Samina. And I'm Kiki.'

'Hi, Kiki. What an unusual name.'

'You're right. I don't know what my mum and dad were thinking!'

Crying starts up behind the curtain.

'I'm sorry, Kiki. I'd better pop back and see to him.'

'No problem.'

She comes back with a child on her hip. Ugly looking kid.

'This is Ramzan. Say "Hello" to the lady, Ramzan.'

Naturally, he turns away.

'He's not usually so shy. Are you, baby? Aren't you going to say "Hello"?'

He twists his head round even further.

'I guess he's tired.' She strokes his hair. 'So, Kiki. What can I get you?'

'Oh, just a couple of things. By the way, are you on Facebook?'

'Facebook? Uhm, no. No, I'm not. I'm not into all that internet stuff.'

'Pity.' I give her a long look, focused mostly on her lips. 'Okay, I'll take two of these, and a pint of semi-skimmed.'

'Do you need a bag?'

'No thanks, Samina.' I graze her fingers as she passes the chocolate bars to me. 'You're very pretty.'

Her eyes widen and she whips back her hand. 'Yes, my husband thinks so.'

I try to grab it again. 'A husband doesn't know what us girls need, Samina. I'll bet yours doesn't.'

She purses her lips and flushes. A deep red, almost burgundy. 'Oh, here he comes now. Rafiq! Rafiq, I need your help with these boxes.'

Hell, she's changed her tune. One minute it's "Hi, Kiki," and the next she's calling for reinforcements. And she's obviously lying about the husband, because he doesn't appear.

'He's not coming, is he, Samina?'

'I think you should leave my shop.'

'But we were just getting to know each other.'

She sets her ugly toddler on its feet and sends it back through the curtain. 'Look, I don't know what you think you're doing, but I want you to leave. Now, please.'

I shrug my shoulders. 'Your loss.'

I won't go back there again. There're plenty of other corners with plenty of other shops. I'm ready for a change, and I don't just mean where I buy my milk. A real change of scene will do me the world of good.

THE REMOVAL VAN'S just gone and I guess I should start unpacking and making this place into a home. I'll just find the kettle first and make a cup of tea. Oh heck, where've I put the teabags? First rule of moving: keep the kettle and teabags handy. Ah, here's the plates and mugs and ...

Who the hell's that at the door? Oh God, please don't give me nosy neighbours. I don't have to answer it; they should know I'm busy. There it goes again. I still can't find the fucking teabags. I may as well go and see who's come to check out the new girl in town.

It was a whole damn family. Three kids, the dad with a short, neat beard, and a pretty young mum wearing a headscarf. I got rid of them quickly, though I did get one of the brats to fetch me some milk. I sent her back again to bring me some sugar.

Oh, sod the unpacking. I've found the DVD player, so I'll just put my feet up for a couple of hours. I always enjoy a good horror movie, night or day.

RIGHT, THAT'S MOST of it sorted. Got my laptop nice and handy on its little table, so I can get onto Facebook and see what's going on in other people's lives. Some of them have got so many friends. How do they do that? Oh, hang on, the cute Muslim wife is locking her front door and going out with the kids. I'm glad I never had kids; so much hard work with all that puking and shitting and crying. No, thank you. Making up lunches and taking them to the park; who in their right mind wants to do that? She's a really pretty girl. The mother, I mean. She must still be in her twenties. And three kids. Three! I bet the husband rapes her every night. She looks quiet and put-upon. I'll try and get to know her soon. Maybe we'd be good for each other. The annoying thing is, I've forgotten her damn name. Can't remember any of them. I think his surname's Ali. Hers is a weird first name, I think. For a good Muslim girl.

I'm still sitting at the window when they get back. I lift the net curtain slightly and give her a wave. She looks embarrassed and turns away to fiddle with the lock. I hope she's not going to be stuck up.

A COUPLE OF WEEKS LATER, when I log onto Facebook, nobody has posted on my wall. I've got six friends, but not one single person, who incidentally, will all have received notifications, has bothered to type in the two little words that would've made all the fucking difference. The big 4-0 and nobody gives a toss. I turn on the DVD player. Perhaps I'll lose myself in one of my favourite movies. Hmm. Yeah, Halloween. The original and the best.

But first I pull the laptop back onto my knee; I can multi-task.

Wow, that was easy! I've created a new email account and got a new friend. And before you can say, 'Way to go, Kiki', he's wishing me Happy Birthday and asking how my day has been. I've called him Myers. Which is quite appropriate, as I'm just watching the scene in Halloween where we first see Michael in his mask.

I HURRY TO ANSWER the knock at the door. 'Oh, hello, neighbour.' Bloody hell, is she blushing?

'I'm sorry to bother you, but do you have a pair of scissors I can borrow? This naughty girl's got chewing gum stuck in her hair and I can't get it out.'

'Yeah, of course. Don't wait on the step, come in.'

'No, I'd better not.'

'Suit yourself.' I hurry to the kitchen and come back with the scissors. 'Keep them for now; I don't need them. And hey, I still don't know your name.'

'It's Polly.' Her voice is as soft as I'm sure her skin must be.

'Well, hello at last, Polly. I'm Kiki. And this one is?'

'Ayesha. Say "Hello" to the nice lady, Ayesha.'

The nice lady! Hmm, I'll take that!

'Hello, Miss Kiki. It's nice to meet you.'

'And you too, Ayesha. Are you a good girl for your amah?'

She grins. 'Sometimes.'

Polly smiles. 'Yes, only sometimes! But you try, don't you, Ayesha?'

'Yes,' she pauses. 'Sometimes! Unless I get chewing gum in my hair!'

'What am I going to do with you?' Polly is laughing.

But I don't see what's so funny about having a cheeky child. 'So, Polly, are you sure you don't have time to come in for a coffee?'

'Oh, thank you, but I can't. My husband will be home soon.'

'Another time then. And hey Polly, I'll hold you to it.'

MY NEW INTERNET FRIENDS are keeping me pretty busy. And Polly, of course. I watch her leave the house with the kids at the same time every day. I follow her sometimes, but it'd be weird if she spotted me, so I don't overdo it. I've accidentally-on-purpose been out sweeping my front step some days when she gets back from the school run. But she's always got some excuse not to come in. The kids are usually skipping around her, jabbering. I can tell she's really sweet and kind though, and I've figured out how to catch her.

'OH HI, POLLY. I'm so glad I've seen you.' I'm looking flustered; hopefully just the right amount. Don't want her to think I'm a total mess and put her off completely. 'Flippin' pakora, I've never been any good at them. Don't suppose you can spare a few minutes to put me right?'

'I don't know, uhm ...'

'Kiki. It's Kiki.'

'Yes, sorry. Kiki.'

Come ON.

'I've just got back from dropping the kids at school, and I've got the cleaning to do, and ...'

I laugh, and try to look vulnerable. 'Help me out, here. Please, Polly. I'm going out to a friend's place later, and I'm out to impress them with my culinary magic!'

'Okay. Just give me a minute and I'll be right over.'

Yessss!

We never do get round to making pakora that day. And we both forget about the make-believe friends I was supposed to be visiting. We talk about everything under the sun. I tell her I have cancer, and I put my arm round her when she tells me her problems with that rat, her husband. I smell her hair – coconut oil, and touch her hand – soft, so soft.

'You're different from all the other women I know, Kiki.'

You'd better believe I am.

'You're so strong. I mean, with the cancer and everything. Where's your husband?'

It rolls off my tongue. 'I'm widowed, Polly.'

'Oh, I'm so sorry.'

'It's a long time ago. But I'd never marry again. Only one person for me.' She doesn't see the look I'm giving her.

'Is that the time? Kiki, I'd better go.'

'It's been nice though, hasn't it? We'll do it again, okay?'

'Yes. That'd be good. Thanks, Kiki.'

As soon as she's gone I pick up her mug and kiss the rim. There's a trace of lipstick on it. I put it back on the coffee table and rinse out my own mug. Then it's down to business. I'm bursting with ideas.

I've decided that the first one I'll use is Skyman. He's Muslim, like Polly. A spirit guide. She'll go for that. I'll take it really slow though. Need to build up some friends for him, and these things take time.

THE NEXT DAY, I'm part-way through setting up the fifteenth profile when I look up and there's Polly herding the kids up her garden path. She looks tired. I want to wave at her. I don't though. I've scared them off in the past, and I'm not risking anything with this one. But hey, she's coming over to me. I'm at the door before she knocks.

'I hope you don't mind me calling on you like this, Kiki. I need to talk to someone.'

'Of course I don't mind. Come in.' I'd rather the kids didn't troop in with her, but what the hell. 'Shoes off, kids. New carpet.'

Along with their mother, two of the kids neatly line up their shoes in the porch. But not that other one!

'Ayesha! Not on the carpet!'

'Sorry, Amah.'

'Is it okay if the kids make a start on their homework, Kiki?'

'Do they get it, at their age? How old are they?'

'Just a little bit. And I like to make sure they get it done. Ayesha's eight now, and ...'

I tune out; I don't care how old the kids are. 'That's fine. They can sit at the living room table.' I shut the door on them and start to make tea for Polly and I.

'I know we hardly know each other, but I don't know where to turn.'

'Oh, Polly. Don't worry. You can tell me anything.'

Her lip quivers and I stifle the urge to run my finger along it.

'It's Afsar. He's so distant these days. I mean, he's never really been a loving man, but now! There's no tenderness; nothing at all.'

I put my arm around her shoulders. 'He could be seeing someone else, honey.'

'Do you think so?'

'I've got a friend. He's a spirit guide. He'll find out for us.'

OF COURSE, SKYMAN does find out that her no-good husband *is* having an affair, and recommends that she relies on her dear friend, Kiki, for support.

And it's true what they say. Time does fly when you're having fun. Polly often pops in for a cup of tea, and we always get together with Skyman for his wisdom and guidance. I wish Polly would come without the brat though. Evil look in her eye, that one.

'How many times? Shoes off in my house, Ayesha.'

'Okay, Miss Kiki.'

'Don't put them on the carpet!'

Polly looks exasperated. 'Leave them in the porch.' She turns to me. 'I can't do anything with her these days, Kiki.'

'Go and sit in the corner, Ayesha. Your mum and I want to talk.'

'Where's your homework? Didn't you bring it? Oh, Ayesha!'

'Never mind, Polly. She can just sit there quietly. Can't you?'

Polly and I go through to the kitchen.

'Afsar's being awful to me again, Kiki. I don't know what to do. He shouted at me in front of the kids, and they started crying, and I was crying and trying to hit him. But he just held onto my wrists and sneered into my face.'

'It keeps on happening, honey. Just like Skyman said it would.'

'Yes, I know.'

'Remember what else he said?'

She glances through the open door at Ayesha. I touch her cheek and turn her face back to me. 'He said you've got to leave him, Polly.'

'I know. I know. But the kids. And, well everything.' She looks so young and lost.

'Our spirit guide knows best. You've got to do it, Polly.'

The tears are coming. That's good.

'Don't wait anymore. It's time to do it. Right now. Hasn't Skyman been saying so for weeks?'

She nods, weakly.

'He wouldn't go to the trouble of sending all those texts if he didn't want you to get out of there and be safe. We've trusted him up to now, and he's never let us down.'

'I know. Oh Kiki, I just can't think straight.'

'You don't need to. That's what Skyman and I are here for. Let us look after you.'

'I want that. I really do.'

Ayesha has come into the kitchen and is tugging at her mother's sleeve.

'What now? Oh, this child! I don't know what to do with her.'

'Ayesha! Why are you such a naughty girl when you know your poor amah is upset?'

'I'm sorry, Miss Kiki. Sorry, Amah.'

'It's not really good enough though, is it? Is it, Ayesha?'

'No, Miss Kiki. But I'm trying to stop being naughty, I really am.'

Stupid brat. That look on her face. As if she's genuinely sorry for all she's done, and she's looking to me to forgive her. As if! All I want to do is punch her.

'Amah, I've got a tummy ache.'

Polly draws the child towards her. 'Why didn't you say so right away, sweetheart?'

No, Polly, no! 'She's faking it, Polly. Can't you see that?'

'No, Amah. My tummy really is sore.'

'Remember what Skyman told us about her lies.'

'Yes, but if she doesn't feel well …'

'Polly! You need to slap her.'

'No! Kiki, I don't hit the children, ever!'

'I'm sorry, but you know I've been getting texts from Skyman telling me that's what we need to do. Especially with Ayesha. It's for her own good.'

'I know. But I can't. I just can't, Kiki.'

'Then we can't expect him to help us anymore. And he'll probably stop helping me with my cancer. He said so.'

Polly looks helplessly around her. Her eyes rest on the brat. 'Did he really say that?'

I decide to forgive her for doubting me, and show her the texts.

'Perhaps, perhaps you could do it, Kiki?'

With great pleasure. 'Well, maybe just this first time. But if we need to discipline her again, you'll have to play your part.'

She looks relieved. 'I will.'

I turn to the brat. 'Ayesha, you don't really have tummy ache, do you?'

'Yes, I …'

'You don't, do you?'

'I, I don't know.' She looks to her mother. 'Amah, why won't you listen to me?'

If I cared a flying fuck about her, I'd be feeling sorry that she looks so confused right now. But I don't. So I slap her face instead. 'That's what you get for telling lies.'

'But, I …'

Whack! A little harder this time. 'You were lying, weren't you, Ayesha?'

Tears are running down her hot little cheeks. 'Yes, Miss Kiki.'

'I can't hear you.'

'Yes, Kiki.'

'Now, will you be good for your amah?'

She nods.

'And it's Aunt Kiki, from now on.'

'Aunt Kiki?'

'Have you gone deaf, girl?'

'No. No, Aunt Kiki.'

They walk back to their house and I grasp the edge of the worktop as I see Polly's arm slip round her daughter's shoulders. I'll have to sort that out.

'HE WANTS US to move away.'

It's like my heart stops beating. And when it starts again I want to go next door and rip Afsar Ali's head right off. 'He won't. He can't. You won't go, will you, Polly? You belong here with me.'

'I don't know what to do. He's a good provider, Kiki.'

'So what! I can look after you, Polly.'

'I know. I know you would. But the kids.'

'I'll take care of all of you. We could be a family. You don't need him.'

'But, I'm his wife, Kiki. Oh, I don't know!'

'Remember what Skyman says, Polly. We can't go against him now.'

A FEW WEEKS LATER, it's done. We're all living together. Can you believe it? She's free. Of him, I mean. She's not really free at all, of course. Because she's mine. And she'll really and truly be mine once Jimmy starts to play his part. If it wasn't for that sly-faced brat of hers trying to come between us, life would be perfect.

I'm taking the next step nice and slow. I've decided it's best to leave it to Skyman to introduce her to Jimmy.

'How does he know Jimmy?' says Polly. 'How does Skyman know he's okay?'

I laugh. 'Well, he certainly looks okay!'

Yesss! That's definitely a blush. 'I know, but ...'

'And Polly, when did Skyman ever let us down?'

'Never. You're right, he's never let us down. But what does he want us to do with Jimmy?'

'He'll tell us when he's ready.'

Polly giggles like a schoolgirl. 'He's very good looking, isn't he?'

I can control my jealousy when I think of my plan. 'Very,' I say.

The kids tumble in and Polly quickly makes them some jam sandwiches.

'Hurry up and finish that, Ayesha.'

'I'm trying, Amah.'

'Your brother and sister finished theirs ages ago,' I say, my lip curling at the sight of jam and crumbs round her stupid mouth. 'Just hurry up.'

Polly sighs. 'It's always you, Ayesha. Every time. Why are you so naughty?'

I frown at the brat. 'Just leave it and go to your room.'

Her mother shakes her head at her daughter's retreating back.

'Forget about her, Polly. Let's just relax and watch a film.'

'Now? It's still light outside!'

'I'll draw the curtains. You choose a film.'

'Vampires or one of the Halloween ones?'

'Hmm, vampires. And you can hold onto me if you get scared.'

She *does* get scared of course, and by the end of the film she's holding onto me for dear life.

To stop myself from holding her too close, I force myself to get up and make a cup of tea. When I bring it to her, she has one of her faraway looks.

'You alright, Pol?'

She hesitates just a moment, then stretches and smiles. 'Yes, I'm fine. Oh gosh, I wonder what the kids are up to? We've left them for ages.'

'They'll be alright. Look, I need you to read this message from Skyman.'

'Okay, let me see. Hmm, it says we need to make a list. Things Ayesha needs to do to be good. Yes, yes that's a great idea! Then she can see where she needs to improve, and she will improve, Kiki. I'm sure of it.'

Not if I have anything to do with it. 'Call her in, Polly.' Even the sound of her footsteps on the stairs cuts right through me.

'Have I been bad again, Amah? I didn't mean to be, I promise.'

'Ayesha!' I know she's scared of me now, and it gives me a glow.

'Please, Aunt Kiki. I'm trying so hard.'

'We're making a list of all the naughty things you do, and when we check it, you'd better have stopped all your bad behaviour.'

'I will, Aunt Kiki. I want to be good.'

'Oh, get up to your room again. I can't stand the sight of you and neither can your amah. Nobody likes you.'

The brat glances at her mother, and I'm so proud of Polly for turning her face away.

'Back to your room! Now!'

'**I CAN'T STOP THINKING** about Jimmy.'

'Of course you can't, honey. Skyman says he's the right man for you.'

'And I agree. I just wish India wasn't so far away.'

'Remember, Skyman is never wrong.'

'And everyone else says he's right for me too.'

I'm not daft; I've got a whole lot of other internet 'friends' that Polly will never meet; all working for me.

'Of course they do. Now Polly, I want to show you Skyman's latest texts. I don't know how you're going to feel about what he says we have to do.' I reach out to her. 'Come here. I want to hold you while you look at them.'

She reads slowly, and I feel her body tense. Eventually she looks up at me. 'You're my truest friend, Kiki. And I love Jimmy. Skyman is showing me the way I can be with Jimmy. But …'

I force myself to stay silent, pasting a questioning look onto my face. Inside I'm praying to a God I don't believe in.

'Oh Kiki, it's wonderful!' She stops and claps her hand to her mouth. 'I'm sorry, Kiki. I got carried away without asking you what you think about it.'

'Let me see them again. I didn't really follow them the first time.' I look grave and pretend to read the texts carefully. 'Is he really saying that we have to sleep together? That I'm to be your connection to Jimmy? Oh Polly, I don't know.'

She clasps her hands and says nothing.

I look at the screen again. 'Is that what he's saying, Polly? Oh, I don't know, I don't know.' Oscar for Kiki!

'Please, Kiki. It's the only way Jimmy and I can be together.'

'Through me.'

131

'Yes. I know it's a lot to ask, but ...'

'I'll do it. I'll do it for you, Polly. But just leave me alone for a few minutes to think it through.'

I wait in the lounge for as long as I can bear, but I can't leave her for too long. I don't want her having second thoughts. I go back into the kitchen, phone in hand. 'Skyman's texted again.' I pass her the phone.

'Tonight!' she says. 'But yes, he's right. Why wait? And I want to be with Jimmy so much.'

I NEVER THOUGHT I could be this happy. Polly shares my bed and believes she's making love to Jimmy. The two good kids are seen and not heard, and Polly's become quite adept at beating Ayesha with the wooden spoon. Surprising what an innocent kitchen utensil can do. And I think she's starting to hate her as much as I do. Starting to believe she's an evil little witch who doesn't deserve to be loved.

But it isn't enough. We need to do more to punish her. Like I told my friend on the phone the other day; I actually feel I could kill her.

I'VE MADE POLLY bite her, like a vampire, and tell her she hates her. The kid looks horrified at that! Polly beats her for the slightest thing now, and we hear her crying in her room every evening. My favourite though, is when one of us puts the mask on and bursts into her room in the middle of the night. Does the stupid girl really not know it's me or her mother? By the way she screams and shits herself she doesn't seem to. I'm perfecting a pretty terrifying voice to go with it. Turns out I'm quite the actor. Definitely missed my calling.

Sometimes I think Polly's as daft as the brat. She actually believes we're scaring the evil out of the girl.

'OH KIKI, how on earth are we going to get through the school holidays with Ayesha misbehaving all the time?'

'Hmm, it's not going to be easy. Did you see how long she took to eat her sandwich yesterday? And now she's wetting herself nearly every day!'

'I know. I'm sorry, Kiki. The other two are fine. But Ayesha!'

'She's not only hurting you and me, Polly. She's hurting Jimmy and all our friends.'

'I know, I know. But I just can't beat her any harder, Kiki. You know, like Skyman suggested.'

'It seems to be the only answer, Polly. And listen, I wasn't going to tell you this, but Skyman says she's making my cancer flare up again.'

'No! Oh no, Kiki.'

'She's evil, Polly. We both know that. So we have to beat the devil out of her.'

'Kiki, I'm so sorry. She's just getting worse and worse, isn't she? I don't know why she's changed so much.'

'Let's just wait for the next text from Skyman and we'll do whatever he tells us to do. How does that sound?'

'Yes, we'll do that. He'll know what to do.'

'Doesn't he always?'

She nuzzles closer to me. 'Yes. What am I worrying about?'

'You're such a silly girl at times!'

'I know. I don't know how you put up with me.'

Unsurprisingly, Skyman comes up with the goods in the time it takes Polly to make a cup of tea.

She repeats the words of the text. 'As hard as we can.'

'We agreed to abide by whatever he said.'

'Yes, of course. Skyman is right.'

'It's your turn, Polly.'

'Yes, in a minute.'

'Go now, Polly.'

I make sure the door is open a crack so I can hear the brat's cries.

'Amah, please Amah, I'm trying my best. I don't want to be bad.'

I manage to remove the smile from my face by the time Polly comes back.

'She's wet herself again, Kiki.'

I sigh, and get up from the chair. 'Did you run the bath?'

'Yes, it's running now. But Kiki, shouldn't we add just a little bit of warm water?'

'Skyman said cold, honey.'

THE SUMMER HOLIDAYS are almost over, when one Wednesday afternoon I enter the kitchen, where the brat is making her usual mess of washing the dishes. 'Ayesha!'

'Yes, Aunt Kiki?'

Oh, the terror all over her face. Utterly delicious; I almost clap my hands. 'I have just checked the bathroom. You have not cleaned it exactly as I instructed you to.'

'I'm sorry, Aunt Kiki. I'll do it again when I've finished in here.'

I whack her. 'You'll do it when I say so. And I say you do it now!'

'I'm so tired, Aunt Kiki. And hungry too.'

'What! What did you say, you ungrateful girl!'

'I said … Nothing, Aunt Kiki.'

Polly comes into the kitchen. 'What is she doing now?'

'Have you seen the bathroom she has supposedly scrubbed clean?'

'Ayesha, what is the matter with you? Can't you do as you're told?'

'Get upstairs,' I say. 'And later you can write down everything you have done wrong today.'

'Yes, Aunt Kiki. But I'm so hungry. Amah, can I please have a drink and a biscuit before I go?'

'Your amah agrees with me, Ayesha.'

Polly nods. Good girl.

'It's a cold bath for you, Ayesha,' I say. 'For your useless attempt to clean the bathroom.'

I don't need to coach Polly very much these days. She drags the brat by an arm and her hair, and Ayesha sobs as they thump up the stairs. I follow behind them.

'Kiki, shall I put in a little warm water?'

'Of course not! Why do you have to ask me that? You know Skyman's instructions as well as I do.'

'Yes, you're right. I'm sorry.'

Ayesha flails her arms and legs, as her mother pushes her in, and Polly is soon almost as wet as the brat.

'Keep still, Ayesha!' I yell at her.

Her teeth are chattering, but she tries her best to stop thrashing around. When I shove her head under the water, she begins to struggle again.

'Hold her, Polly.'

'But ...'

'Have you forgotten *everything* Skyman said?'

Water splashes everywhere as we push her down, and with a glance at Polly I grab the shower head and bash the brat with it.

'You do it too, Polly.'

She takes it from me obediently. She doesn't beat her as hard as I do, but it's soon my turn again.

'Should we stop now, Kiki?'

I couldn't stop if I wanted to. 'No, we have to hit her harder.' *Wow, what a feeling!* 'Come on, Polly. Grab something else you can beat her with.' I've never felt this good. The power to tell another woman to do this to her own child. And the child so absolutely terrified, screaming its head off when it comes up for air. I never want it to stop.

I crash the metal down on her stupid head again and again, and blood is pouring into the water. Then her eyes seem to cross and she goes limp.

Polly turns to me in horror. 'No! Oh, Kiki, what have we done?'

'Don't worry about it, Polly. We've only done what we had to do.'

'But, oh Kiki, I think she's … she's …'

I wish Polly would be quiet. 'Skyman told us to beat her. So we beat her. We've done nothing wrong.'

'But … Ayesha! Ayesha sweetheart, wake up!'

Why won't Polly shut up? The stupid bitch is spoiling the moment.

An Overview of Ayesha's Case

Ayesha Ali

13.12.04 - 28.08.13

aged 8 years & 8 months

London, England

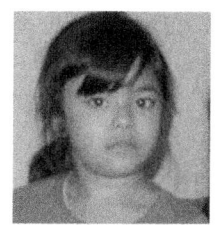

One of the many reasons for including Ayesha's story in this volume, is to highlight the incredible web of deceit spun, via social media, by Kiki Muddar. Nowadays, only nine years later, this could not happen on quite the same scale, as on Facebook at least, each user is limited to one account. This change is due, wholly or in part, to the gross misuse of multiple accounts, and possibly by Ayesha's case in particular. (I cannot trace the source in order to verify this as fact.)

Ayesha's torment began when a new neighbour, Kiki Muddar, moved in next door to her family, and became obsessed with her mother, Polly Chowdhury. Polly's husband, Afsar Ali, stated that prior to meeting Kiki Muddar, his wife had been a loving mother, but when the marriage broke down, and the couple separated, Muddar invaded Polly's world unhindered.

Chowdhury was a straight woman, and Muddar wanted her as a sexual partner, so she pretended she had cancer to gain Polly's sympathy, whilst also gradually building up a labyrinth of fake internet personae to reel the younger woman in. One of Muddar's invented personae was a man she named Jimmy, who 'lived' in India. Through a long grooming process and hundreds of thousands of messages, Polly fell in love with Jimmy, and was convinced by the older woman that via sex with Muddar, Polly was making love to Jimmy. Elated with the control she found she could wield over Polly, Muddar also manipulated her into persecuting her own daughter, who she felt stood in the way of Polly's total devotion to her. The principal persona in this part of Muddar's plan was 'Skyman', who she put forward as a 'spirit guide'. Through Skyman, and a myriad of other fake characters, Muddar led Polly to believe that her daughter was evil, to the extent of being possessed by demons. Muddar then induced Polly to join her in punishing Ayesha, supposedly to drive the evil away.

Investigators found a number of lists, written by Ayesha, in an attempt to 'become good', so that she could avoid the punishments she had begun to receive. The little girl's lists were set out in two columns, with one side for good things she would try to do, including 'Finishing my jam sandwich on time' and 'Being quick in the bathroom' and the other side for things she felt had angered the two main adults in her life, including 'Whinging and making a fuss' and 'Ignoring someone' and 'Not putting my shoes in the right place'.

Another note Ayesha wrote shows how much she blamed herself, felt isolated from her friends, and was desperately trying to change, in order to please Kiki and her mother.

Heart-breakingly, at the bottom of this letter (see overleaf), there is a sentence which has been crossed out, which reads 'Amah (mother) loves me, but does not like me. I am crying right now'.

The whole letter reads:

Nothing has changed at all! And I'm not just letting myself down, but I am letting my family and Kiki down as well. It's the weekend today and most of my friends are probably having a laugh, watching telly, whereas I am just sitting here making notes! I'm soooooooooo bored. As you can see, I have written a lot. But I am just writing to myself. I have learnt while I am sitting here, that I have to change! I WILL CHANGE, NO MATTER WHAT! If I be rude then nobody will like me! Being thought bad, naughty and mean, it's getting to be very upsetting. I don't like hurting other people's feelings! I don't know how I make myself do these things! I hate getting punishments so I'm gonna make sure I change. Amah loves me but does not like me. I am crying right now.

!! Nothing has changed at all! And I'm not just letting myself down, but, I am letting my family and Kiki down as well. It's the weekend today and most of my friend are probably having a laugh, watching telly, where as I am just sitting here making notes. I'm soo ooooooooooo bored. As you can see, I have written a lot. But, I am just writing to myself. I have learnt, while I am sitting here, that I have to change! I WILL CHANGE, NO - MATE WHAT! If I be rude then nobody will like me! Being thought bad, naughty and mean it's getting to be very upsetting. I don't like hurting other people's feelings! I don't know how I make myself do these things! I hate getting punishments so I'm gonna make sure I change.

Punishments included not giving Ayesha enough to eat, shutting her up in her room, and making her scrub the house. Her mother also beat Ayesha both with her hand and a wooden spoon, and Muddar gave her cold baths as punishment for wetting the bed (which as we know, often occurs when a child is frightened). With chilling cruelty, the two women would also put on scary horror masks (they were both horror film fanatics) in the middle of the night, to terrify the little girl. Muddar also convinced Chowdhury that Ayesha had 'bad blood' which was making her fake cancer worse.

During the school summer holidays of 2013, the cruelty and violence to Ayesha escalated, and six months after Polly and her family began sharing a household with Muddar, her eight year old daughter was dead.

Ayesha had more than 50 injuries all over her body, including at least one human bite mark, multiple bruises, and carpet burns. The fatal blow was dealt when one of her killers bashed her over the head with a shower head. When Kiki Muddar's phone call brought the paramedics to the Chadwell Heath home, she told them that Polly had murdered her daughter and tried to kill herself. (Indeed, a series of notes were found, written by Chowdhury, saying: 'I have taken my life and Ayesha's life'.)

When paramedic Laura Ward asked Muddar if she was concerned about Ayesha, she replied: 'She was a naughty child and Mum thought she was possessed by the devil.' Muddar, later deemed to have narcissistic personality disorder, showed no feeling at all for the little girl.

Ayesha's story is so bizarre and convoluted that it took the police many months of determined searching to unravel the web of more than 100,000 texts and social media messages that Muddar had spun to entrap Chowdhury and torture her daughter. Their endeavours paid off when they found that none of the many characters existed, except in Muddar's mind. The so-called lover, Jimmy, was an innocent man from India with no knowledge of Chowdhury or Muddar, whose photo the latter had used.

Along with the thousands of saved texts, Muddar kept recordings of all her phone calls from the beginning of 2013, some of which were given in evidence at the trials at the Old Bailey. As Ayesha's father wept, the recording of a phone call, between Muddar and a friend, which took place a month before the murder, was played. Muddar calls Ayesha a witch, and speaks repeatedly about killing the little girl, insisting that she wasn't joking. Although many of the friend's responses are inaudible, and it's possible that she does try to dissuade Muddar (advising her to go out for a walk), she asks Muddar why *Ayesha* (my italics) is acting so crazy. Muddar continues her expletive filled rant, saying that Ayesha shits the bed, and repeats that she is evil. Given the threats Muddar is making, her friend's last words are peculiar: *Okay, yeah. Let me know what you do.*

A neighbour testified that she had heard Ayesha screaming, and crying out to her mother, 'Amah, I don't want to be bad. Amah, Amah, I don't want to be bad.'

DI Convery of the Metropolitan Police said that 'Ayesha was a bright and intelligent little girl who was well liked by teachers and classmates alike'. In contrast, the instigator of her cruel murder, Kiki Muddar, was described by Judge Christopher Moss QC as a 'manipulative and wicked' woman, who subjected the child to a 'life of cruelty and misery that defies belief'.

Both women were found guilty of manslaughter, with Chowdhury being handed down a thirteen year sentence, and Muddar eighteen years. These were reduced on appeal to ten and fifteen years respectively.

Whilst Kiki Muddar's use of the internet may seem outlandish, we are beginning to see many instances of social media playing a role in abusers communicating their plans to punish the child in their 'care'. We even see evidence, on Youtube and the like, of so-called parental discipline taking place.

Thank you to Freya for alerting me to Ayesha's story

Rest Safely in Peace, Ayesha

Technology and the Media

Kiki Muddar is not the only abuser to use technology in her campaign of terror against her victim, and with the media, in all its forms, now playing a huge part in our lives, the use of technology by murderers is contributing to their downfall.

Footage from cameras, set up in various rooms in an abusive household, to ensure the victim is obeying orders, can now be brought in as clear evidence when the perpetrators are brought to trial.

The tortures of Takoda Collins, and of Adrian Jones, whose almost unbelievable stories I cover in later volumes, were recorded in this way.

Texts exchanged by the murderers of Daniel Pelka, Gabrielle Barrett, Arthur Labinjo-Hughes, and many others, exposed their crimes in court and strengthened the case for the prosecution.

And whilst it did not save Omaree Varela (in the next story) from his suffering, the recording of the phone call to the police, and the footage from the lapel camera of the officers, clearly implicates his murderers. CCTV also captures abuse outside the the home, such as the water torture of a seven year old boy, which was filmed by a passer-by, and has given me sleepless nights, imagining the suffering he was enduring at home.

News media is a double-edged sword. Often portraying child murderers as monsters (which in many eyes, they are), they then move on to blaming those who failed to help the victim, such as child protection agencies, whipping up the general public into a frenzy that does little to protect children from harm.

But when a child is missing, news and social media can be helpful when asking for, or disseminating, information.

In an example from the 1980's, when the birth mother of Dennis Jurgens became convinced that his adoptive mother had murdered him, no one believed her. Only when she turned to the press did she find herself taken seriously, and with their support, she uncovered the truth. I tell Dennis' story in Volume 3.

Social media has become a place where family members, whose cries for help fell on deaf ears, can reach out to others in the same position.

On Facebook, there are numerous groups for those directly affected by child murder, and those who support them in their fight for justice, working towards changes in the law, and fair sentences for the perpetrators.

JESSICA JACKSON

Invitation To My Readers' List

The children's stories continue in a moment, but first, I hope you'll be interested in this ...

If you share my passion to protect children, and would like to join my Readers' List, I'd love to welcome you by sending you a **FREE ebook**.

You will then gain access to **members only offers**, including the chance to receive an exclusive, **personally signed paperback book**, each new release at the subscriber price, special offers on similar books, and lots more.

Sound good?

Just pick up your free ebook and join us!

Details on the next page ...

Pick Up Your Free E-Book

Isaiah Torres was just six years old when he was abused to death in the most appalling way.

Don't miss this book, in which I also include bonus content about Baby Brianna Lopez.

Just scan this code:

Or use this link:

https://BookHip.com/KXACJDT

See overleaf to enter my draw …

Enter My Draw

After you've joined us, I'll email you with an invitation to enter the draw for a members' exclusive **personally signed paperback book and bookmark**; UNIQUE only to winners of the draw.

 **Please don't miss the chance to enter, by being sure to check your Inbox, Junk or Spam, and you can also add my email address to your Contacts, and your safe sender / VIP list.**

jessicajackson@jesstruecrime.com

(If you have problems signing up, just email me, and I'll be happy to add you manually.)

Good luck in the draw!

And by the way ...

Thanks To You

When you buy one of my books, read pages in KU, write a review, or tell your friends about my books, you are not only helping to raise awareness, but to raise money for child protection charities.

I donate royalties from my books to these three charities:

– NSPCC (UK)

– UNICEF (worldwide)

– Prevent Child Abuse America (US)

Let's carry on with the children's stories

The Best of Everything

Martina

'HEY, MARTINA, LOOK OUT!' laughed Sylvia. 'You're gonna squeeze him half to death!'

I tickled her little nephew's tummy. 'Sorry, Sylvia. He's just so darn cuddly. Aren't you, Omaree?'

The toddler grinned up at us.

'I guess he is,' said Sylvia. 'I can't help myself either!'

Omaree squealed with delight as his auntie Sylvia picked him up for a cuddle.

'Who's got the biggest brown eyes in New Mexico?'

Omaree pointed to his chest.

'And the curliest hair?'

'Me! Me!'

'You sure have,' I said. 'Oh, Sylvia, I miss my own kid.'

'I know, hun. You get yourself a job and get straightened out, and you'll soon have her back.'

'I sure hope so.'

I'd just turned sixteen and things hadn't always been easy for me. My stepdad used to lay on me when Mom was out at work, and when I told, nobody believed me. After I grew big, they took my baby away, and I went pretty wild until Sylvia and David took me in. They were the best guardians ever. I loved their kids and helped out where I could, but Sylvia kept telling me to try and find a real job so I could get on my own two feet, and get my little girl back. I knew she was kinda worried I'd end up getting wasted like her kid sister Synthia; Omaree's mom.

WE SAW SYNTHIA downtown one day. Man, she looked rough.

'Hey, Synthia.'

'Oh yeah, hey Sylvia. Hi Martina.'

'How's it going, sis? You don't look so good.'

'Going great. Fantastic. Matter of fact I'm about ready to get my little boy back. Hey, Omaree.'

I didn't like her touching him with those filthy, jagged fingernails. And Omaree seemed to shrink back from her.

'I'll come and get you, son. And we'll be a proper family.'

'You still with that Steve Casaus?' said Sylvia.

'Sure am. He's a great guy. I never got why you don't like him.'

'It's the drugs, sis. You know that.'

'We're clean, man! Why does nobody believe that?'

'Anyways, we gotta go now. You look after yourself. And don't worry about Omaree. We love having him.'

As we walked away, I whispered to Sylvia, 'She sure don't *look* clean.'

'My sister hasn't been clean since she was sixteen!'

We walked along the path through the park, swinging Omaree between us.

'What happened to her, Sylvia? I thought you said you were brought up real well.'

'Yeah, we had a good childhood, y'know. Really happy. Kinda privileged, I guess. Mom and Dad worked overseas and we went with them. Visited Europe and everywhere. We both did well in school too.'

I did my best to hide how envious I felt.

'But when we came back, bam! She found meth and lost herself.'

'That sucks.' Huh, she had a good start in life and then she blew it. I wished I'd had her chances.

'By the time she turned eighteen she was living with a drug dealer and having her first kid. She couldn't take care of him so our mom and dad took him, and he's been doing great ever since.'

'And then she had Omaree. And you're taking care of him!' I stroked his head. 'Hey, Sylvia ... '

'Yeah?'

'Please don't let her have him back.'

'They won't let her take him. The state she's in. And I've got papers giving me custody. Don't worry, Martina.'

Omaree put his arms up, wanting me to carry him.

'No, Omaree, you gotta keep walking. He's getting kinda plump, Sylv; I don't think I can lift him.'

Sylvia laughed. 'I'm not sure you've got a choice, Martina.'

Omaree was grinning up at me. He was wearing a cute baseball cap back to front. He knew he had me under his thumb. I reached down and kissed him, and his grin worked its way up to a chuckle.

'You'll be a great mom,' said Sylvia. 'You'll get your little girl back.'

'Some day.' I fought back the tears, as usual. 'Hey, it's hard to believe this cheeky fella was born in jail.'

'Yeah, Grant's Correctional. I think it was for trafficking drugs that time.'

I kissed little O again, and he planted his lips on my arm. Oh God, I could've eaten him up.

THAT NIGHT, I couldn't stop thinking about Synthia. Sylvia had told me that after she got released from jail, she had Omaree stay with a whole bunch of people. One of them was Essie. I knew Essie. Kids everywhere but always had space for one more. She fed me a good meal a time or two when I had nowhere to go. A true friend to Synthia and Sylvia too.

The last time the cops took Synthia off the streets and threw her in jail, Sylvia and David took Omaree to live with them. He was kinda skinny at first, but Sylvia soon got him to put a bit of meat on his bones. It helped that David always held down a job, and he worked real hard, so even though there were six mouths to feed, and then when I turned up and made it seven, nobody ever went hungry. They treated us the same as their own kids and I reckon it was my happiest time, and I knew for sure it was Omaree's.

JUST A FEW NIGHTS LATER, the kids were in bed, and Sylvia, David and me were yawning and about ready to go up ourselves, when somebody started battering on the door and shouting through the crack in the woodwork.

'Open up, Sylvia! I've come to take Omaree back.'

We all looked at each other. After that day we'd seen Synthia downtown we knew this was coming, but just not quite so soon. She'd looked so strung out, and Omaree was doing fine with us; three years old, plump as a peach, and as full of smiles and mischief as Sylvia and David's own kids.

'Go away, Synthia,' Sylvia shouted back. 'It's late. We can talk about this tomorrow.'

We heard some scuffling, then a deep male voice. 'Open up, please ma'am. It's the police.'

'She's got the cops with her,' said Sylvia. 'Oh God, what's that sister of mine up to now?'

'Open up before we get inside our own way.'

'I'll get it, honey,' said David. 'Don't worry.' He eased open the door. It was raining hard outside. 'It's pretty late to come calling, Officer. Can't we talk this through in the morning?'

'I'm sorry, sir. This lady is here to take her child back. And we're here to make sure that happens. I believe your wife here has refused to comply with the court order.'

'Court order?' said David, turning to his wife. 'Sylvia, what's going on?'

'No, they can't take him. We've got the papers.'

'I'm sorry, sir, ma'am. But we've got the legal right to take the child away with us tonight.'

'I've got the documents, sir. My sister's an addict. She can't take care of him.'

Synthia's voice rose above the sound of the pelting rain. 'You godamn bitch, Sylvia. So high and mighty with your perfect family. Well, Omaree is my son, and I want him back.'

Water is dripping from the policemen's caps. 'May we come in please?'

David sighed and let the two officers over the threshold. 'She stays outside,' he told them. 'She'll upset the kids.'

But Synthia wasn't giving up. 'Let me in out of the rain. Please, Syl,' she said. 'I'm half-drowned already.'

'If she promises to stay down here and behave herself, I guess she can come in too,' said Sylvia. 'I'll get the papers, Officer. Just give me a minute.'

As the intruders shook the rain off their jackets, Sylvia rummaged for the document her sister had signed giving them custody of Omaree, and gave it to the two officers.

'I'm afraid this document is not legal, ma'am. Please go and get the boy.'

Sylvia turned pale and began to sway, and David had to catch her. 'Not legal? You're wrong; you must be wrong. It has to be a mistake.'

'I'm sorry ma'am. There's no mistake. That piece of paper ain't worth squat. Now, are you going to get the boy or not?'

We couldn't move. Sylvia and David had been so confident they had the law on their side. But the officers pushed past us, and soon there was crying from the bedrooms.

'Can I go up, Sylvia?' I asked.

She nodded, and I raced after the cops. 'Wait, I'll get him. He's only three years old; you'll scare him. Let me do it.'

I looked down at Omaree as he lay in his crib. He was the only one of the kids still asleep. My heart lurched at the sight of his gorgeous brown curls. 'Can I have a moment to wake him? Please?'

The cops nodded and headed downstairs again. 'Don't be long now.'

The other kids came sleepily from their beds and crowded round Omaree and me.

'What's happening, Martina?' said the oldest boy. 'I heard the cops with Aunt Synthia. They're not going to take little O, are they? They can't do that, can they?'

I gently eased Omaree up from his bed. 'I know, I know. Don't worry, this'll get straightened out and he'll be back with us before you know it.' I nuzzled his neck, and he gave a little whimper. With all the kids clamouring to kiss him, he suddenly opened his eyes, and gave one of his most beautiful smiles. Then I held him close, and whispered into his ear. 'Don't worry, little O. We're here. We love you.'

We all trooped down the stairs.

Sylvia was pleading with the cops. 'He won't be safe with her, Officer. She's on crack. So's her skanky boyfriend. They'll hurt him. They've done it before.' She grabbed Omaree from my arms and cried into his neck. 'Please, please, I'm begging you. Don't take him.'

Only Omaree looked happy; loving being the centre of attention. 'Don't cry, Mommy,' he said to Sylvia, and I saw Synthia bristle with rage.

'I'm sorry, ma'am,' said one of the officers.

'Just a few more minutes. Please.'

David eventually had to prise Omaree out of Sylvia's arms and hand him to the officer. Only then did Omaree start to look frightened. 'Mommy! Daddy!'

'*I'm* your Mommy, Omaree,' yelled Synthia.

Omaree screamed as she approached him, and even the officers looked uncertain.

Sylvia tried one last time. 'He's not safe with her. Please, please don't take him. Oh, God, help him.'

But the officers flung open the door and the rain blew in. And Omaree was gone.

Sylvia and David let the kids come into their bed, just like it was a Sunday morning. Even I went in that night, and we all hugged each other, crying. Finally, the oldest two staggered back to their rooms, and the youngest fell asleep in our arms.

I never used to pray. But I prayed for Omaree that night.

Carlos

MY WIFE'S INSISTING on mobile phones for the kids. I think they're too young for them, but I guess I know what she means; there's been some trouble down our way lately, and I want my girls to be safe. And so I'm despatched to the store.

Jeez, it's hot today. I jump out of the pick-up and hope the aircon is working in the mall. Okay, so three phones. I check my wallet; this is not going to be a cheap visit. I'm just gonna browse up and down a little, hope no one bothers me.

Seems to be a trailer trash family in the next aisle. Kids whining, Mom losing her shit over something. Them kids should be in school anyways. Better make my way over to the phones, get to the back of the store where it's quieter. Now, I wonder if they'd do a deal on this little Nokia. Oh sheesh, the woman with the kids from hell has followed me over here. Still, better get on with what I came to do. Keep it down, woman, for chrissake. What's she going on about? Hey, hey don't slap that kid! I look at the family more closely now. The oldest child looks about seven, eight maybe. Skinny, with a haunted look. The younger two got a bit more flesh on their bones.

'What did I tell you?' She's yelling at the skinny kid. 'You're getting nothing. And you know why?

Because you're fucking useless. Worth nothing to me or nobody. No wonder Steve hates you.'

I didn't hear it but I guess the kid must've said something in reply.

'Well, you better start listening real soon. You hear me? You hear me, Omaree?'

I hear her slap him again. I hate to know a kid's being hit. But I put my head down and examine the fancy pink cases I think my girls might like.

'You think you can treat me and Steve this way? You know you can't, but you keep right on pushing our buttons, just waiting for one of us to crack. Well, I gotta tell you, son, Steve is gonna be very interested to know just how you've been behaving today. Omaree, are you listening to me?'

I catch a glimpse of the boy's face. Terrified. He says something I can't hear.

Whack. She's punched him right in the head. And again. By the time I've rounded the end of the aisle she's got him pinned up against the wall, her hands round his neck.

'Now look here, lady ...'

'Don't you "look here" me,' she spits. 'If I need to discipline my kid, I'll do it. And I'll do it where, when and how I want!' But she lets him go.

'You can't do that. What the hell did the kid do anyway?' I immediately wish I hadn't said that. As if he could've done anything to deserve being half strangled.

'You don't know, Mister. You don't wanna know.' She shakes her head. 'You got kids?'

I don't want to be her friend or confidant. 'I sure do. And I never raise a hand to any one of them.'

'You're lucky, sir. This boy of mine, ah Jesus.'

I try to give the kid a supportive look. One that says 'Hang in there. Things'll get better.'

They troop away up the aisle, but the skinny kid turns back and gives me a look that says 'thank you' and 'please help me', both at the same time. But what can I do? I go back to my choice between shocking pink and purple glitter.

The mother of the year can't seem to get more than a few steps before she has the urge to slap her son again. Other shoppers are looking horrified as she attacks him with a powerful fist. I've had enough. I take out my phone and call 911.

'I've called the cops, lady,' I say. 'So you might want to lay off that child.'

She comes right up to me and jabs her finger in my face. 'Like I said. My kid. My rules. My punishment. You got that, Mister?'

I grab the kid's hand, and put myself between him and his mom. 'It's Omaree, right? Don't worry, son. We'll put a stop to this.'

'You can't touch my kid. I'll have you arrested!'

I hold up my hand and tell her not to come any closer. When I drop my arm to my side, I feel Omaree's hand find mine again, and I smile down at him.

'Where do you live, buddy?'

'Don't you dare say nothing, Omaree. This creep's after you. He wants what's in your pants.'

I shake my head. 'Lady, I just want the kid to be safe.'

'If my kids don't behave they know what they'll get, Mister. And there's nothing you can do about it.'

I need to keep her talking till the cops come. 'This is how you want to bring up your kids, is it? Make them terrified of you?'

'Oh, so you want to see terrified? You come to my house when my husband gets home.' She laughs. 'Then you'll see them scared shitless.'

I'm relieved when two officers appear in the doorway. I have to let Omaree go and stand by his mother.

Her transformation is impressive. 'Good afternoon, Officer. I was obliged to scold my son for touching all the merchandise right here. Folks don't want his sticky fingers all over their goods.'

I step forward. 'It was me who made the call, Officer.'

'Thank you, sir.' He turns back to the woman. 'This gentleman says you've been a mite heavy handed with your boy, ma'am.'

'I never laid a finger on him, sir. Omaree, tell the officer how I discipline you kids.'

I hear the boy speak for the first time. Well rehearsed. 'You explain if we do something wrong, Mom.'

'And do I get physical?'

His moment's hesitation should be enough to alert the cop. 'No, Mom.' He's looking straight at me with those big eyes.

'But I witnessed it, Officer,' I say, looking around for the other shoppers, who seem to have dissolved into thin air. 'Tell them, Omaree. No one's gonna hurt you, buddy.'

The cop wedges his hands onto his hips and looms over the kid. 'Son, you sure you're telling the truth? This gentleman right here tells it different to you and your mom.'

The boy hangs his head. 'It's the truth, sir.'

That seems to satisfy the law enforcement officer. 'Mind you treat your kids good, ma'am.'

'Oh I do, Officer.'

I watch them leave; the boy looking pale beneath his olive skin. And scared. As he glances back at me for the last time, he looks scared to death.

Judy

'HI JUDY.'

'Hey Grant. How's it been tonight?'

'Pretty quiet. Been catching up with my studies.'

'How's that coming along?'

'Hmm, not bad. But it's time for me to shoot off.'

'Who's the lucky lady?'

'She looks just like you, Judy. But if you won't have me …'

I grin and practically shove him out the door. I'm old enough to be his grandmother. I nod to my fellow dispatchers on my way to the coffee machine. I haven't eaten all day and I can't wait to tuck into my pastrami on rye.

The first two calls are fairly routine. Boys in hoodies mouthing off to their neighbours, hookers on corners they shouldn't be at.

When the third call comes in, I can't quite make out what's happening. No one speaks, unless that's a whisper I hear when I first pick up. Something tells me not to bellow down the phone asking what the problem is.

Suddenly, a male voice shouts. 'NOW! Sit all the way back. These fucking kids, man. I swear I'm gonna lose it one of these days, Synthia. I'm gonna have a nervous breakdown. You make everybody sick around you. I fucking can't stand you. I really wish we could just get rid of you.'

Alrighty then. So one of the kids knows how this goes. And they've called for help. I get onto the patrol guys straight away, and keep the phone line open. It sounds like a kid has spilt a drink while getting into the car, and is being hit.

'Shut up. SHUT THE FUCK UP. I'm not even doing anything to hurt. Quit faking it.'

The man and a woman seem to be arguing over whether the kid's skin is burnt or bruised.

'This doesn't hurt!' The woman is yelling now. 'So don't act like it hurts. It doesn't, does it? You just want attention, right?'

The child murmurs. 'Yes.'

'He's always faking it, Steve, just like I told you.'

Now it's the man again. 'Yeah, fucking hate him. Yeah, beat the fuck out of him. Even your new fucking brother can't stand you. Shut the fuck up before I really fucking pop you hard, man.'

The kid, who's obviously in pain, is repeatedly told off for whining. *Come on, guys, respond. You need to protect this kid.*

'He's a dumb fuck, man. You're a dumb fucking kid, man. Dumb. You ain't never fucking ever learnt nothing. I hate you more than I hate anybody in my whole life.'

The guys are on their way. I sure hope they're listening to this.

'So don't say nothing, cos you don't got nothing to say, cos you don't give a fuck about nobody or nothing. DO YOU? Do you not know how to fucking talk?'

Don't talk. Talk. What's the kid to do?

'Stop crying, man. Get up, man. Okay, give me a hug, man.'

Wha-at? Now he wants the poor kid to give him a hug?

I let my mind wander for a second, and think of my own kids when they were little. How my youngest used to count the hugs I gave him, and if I came up short that day, we'd have hug-time in the evening. But I'm soon jerked back to reality.

'Really I just want you to be happy. I want you to try. Why don't you wanna try? I don't understand. You don't have to be scared or nothing in your house.'

Then words I can't believe I'm hearing. 'I'm not never gonna hurt you, neither is Mom. We love you, we just want the best for you. Don't you understand that?'

A tiny voice. 'Yes.'

'I want the best for you. The best of everything …'

Omaree

WE'VE JUST GOT BACK from Burger King when the officers ride up.

They heard it! They must've heard the call!

Mom greets them with a smile. 'Can I help you, Officers? Don't keep us too long though, cos the kids are tired. We just got back from the restaurant. We had a great time, didn't we, kids?'

My legs are shaking and my tummy growls because I wasn't allowed to eat at the diner. Mom coughs to cover the sound.

'Been any yelling or anything going on?'

'Yelling? Us? No, except like, the neighbours, they're always fighting and stuff. I guess you mean them? They're drunk all the time.'

'The hit off the cell phone shows a call coming from here.'

'Oh, that. Yeah, my baby was playing with my phone. Where's my phone?'

Oh no, the phone! Will they they know it was me that made the call?

There's no point in hiding it. 'I think I know where it is,' I whisper.

'That's good, son,' says Mom. 'Go and get it.'

I place it on the little stool; out of everyone's reach.

The officer faces Mom squarely. 'Now, we've been told that the recording from the phone shows people yelling and abusing their kids.'

Mom scoffs. 'No, not at all. All that happened was my little girl got out of her seat belt to pass me a soda and it spilled all down my top. She knows she shouldn't get out of the seat belt, and I told her it's dangerous and she shouldn't do that. I don't want my kids to get hurt.'

Heck, Mom's good at this stuff. She sounds like she really cares.

'Was there something about you guys saying I wish you were never my kid?'

So they definitely have listened to the call. I'm trying to catch the tall one's eye. Let him know it was me.

'Sometimes,' Mom nods across at my stepfather. 'He gets stressed out and says he wishes we'd never had kids. But he loves them to death.'

They're bound to notice something's not right. Both Mom and Steve are wasted. They look it, too.

Come on guys, please help us.

Mom's telling the cops that Steve is fussy about his cars, and how he makes us keep the house clean too. She's right about that. But though Steve shouts a lot and gets in your face, it's Mom who loses it when she takes that crack stuff.

You shouldn't have to be scared of your Mom.

Everybody seems to be talking at once. I pray to Jesus that the tall guy will take me off into another room and ask me questions I can answer truthfully. But Mom is talking and talking about health insurance and other stuff. Suddenly the cops are saying we seem like good people, and Mom and Steve should be careful of the things they say.

'Steve can get a little loud at times, and seem quite dominant,' says Mom.

'We have to get a little like that in our jobs. So we understand that,' says one of the cops. 'It can seem aggressive, I guess.'

My baby brother plays with Mom's cell phone, and it makes the grownups laugh. I try a smile. But I know that when the officers have gone, and Mom realises who made that 911 call, she won't be laughing.

The cops are talking to my stepdad. Say they appreciate him being honest. I think maybe they didn't hear the call after all.

'You seem like a good family, but you got to be careful, you know. If people hear things, you could get in trouble, you know.'

As they're leaving, Mom asks the officers if she's doing right by getting me to do yard work, raking up and stuff, because the neighbours had been giving her hell about it. The cops tell her she's being very responsible doing that, and that I'll grow up nice and strong. What Mom didn't tell them is that the neighbours saw her punching and kicking me real hard when I didn't work fast enough.

How can I get the cops to stay? Mom and Steve will know it was me who dialled 911. And I don't know what they'll do. I still hurt everywhere from yesterday, and I can't take another beating.

Mom is kinda thanking the cops for stopping by. Like everybody's done a great job and they're proud of themselves. And there's nothing more to be done.

'No worries,' says one of the officers as they get into their vehicle and drive away.

Please don't go. You could take me back to Auntie Sylvia's. That was a long time ago, and I was only a kid, but I still remember. When I was happy. When I was safe.

An Overview of Omaree's Case

Omaree Varela
03.02.04 - 27.12.13
aged 9 years & 8 months
Albuquerque, New Mexico

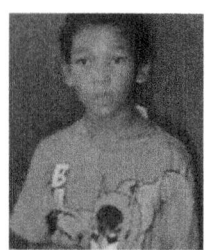

This still photograph is taken from the video recording (from the officer's lapel camera) of the police visit to the Varela residence in June 2013. A few months later, Omaree was kicked to death by his mother, Synthia Varela.

You and I can see how terrified he looks in the photo, but the officers did not. It must have taken a lot of courage for this little boy to make the 911 call that he hoped would save him. But the officers who came that day did not listen to the recording of the call, despite the pleas of the dispatcher to do so. They did not see the fear in his eyes nor speak to Omaree privately. In fact, they did not speak to him at all. Neither did they file a report, nor inform the CYFD (Children, Youth and Family Department). Had they done so, it would have been added to two previously filed substantiated reports, when his teacher spotted an injury on Omaree's face, and when staff and customers in a Cricket phone store witnessed his abuse by his mother. But, no one saved Omaree. When questioned about how he died, Synthia Varela initially claimed that her son had fallen off a toy horse and banged his head. And that she had tried to revive him by taking him into the shower. Varela later changed her story to something nearer the truth, and his mother was eventually found guilty of kicking him to death.

The child's autopsy was carried out by Medical Investigator Sam Andrews MD, who gave the cause of death as blunt trauma, and found multiple injuries at different stages of healing. Dr Andrews reported bruising on the chest, arms, legs and tongue, abrasions on the face, a healing laceration of the scalp, and haemorrhage into the muscles between the ribs, the soft tissues of the back, the diaphragm, abdominal wall, the abdominal cavity, the soft tissues around the pancreas and left kidney, and on the outer surface of the bowel. Injuries consistent with burns were found on Omaree's chest. A bruise on the right forearm was suggestive of a human bite. Omaree had lost 25% of his blood volume as he bled into his abdominal cavity.

When Synthia Varela changed her story about the accident with the rocking horse, she told police that she had knocked him into a dresser. After he fell to the floor, she said she stomped him twice and kicked him in the abdomen. 'I didn't do it. It wasn't intentional. It was an accident. I was disciplining him and I kicked him the wrong way. It was an accident.'

I would just like to repeat that: 'I was disciplining him. I kicked him the wrong way.'

This is *one of the many reasons* that I don't hold with physically disciplining a child. Too many caregivers do not understand what lengths (if any) to go to. Of the hundreds of children abused to death every month, their first experience of 'discipline' has often begun as a tap on the butt, escalating over time to being kicked, beaten, drowned, burned, etc. If the child survives, they learn that violence is the way to deal with everyday occurrences, such as bed-wetting or not finishing a task quickly enough. Those who do not continue this abuse to their own children are heroes in my eyes. The rest simply don't know there are other options, and repeat the cycle.

Synthia Varela pleaded guilty to second degree murder, various child abuse charges, and tampering with evidence and was handed down a 40 year prison sentence.

Stephen Casaus initially claimed he was not at home when his stepson was being murdered, but later admitted that he had been present, shooting up heroin in another room, and had heard Synthia beating her son. Casaus was found guilty of recklessness, in that he did not prevent the abuse that killed Omaree, nor call for help after the beating. For these crimes, and for child abuse, tampering with evidence, bribery and intimidation of witnesses, the judge sentenced Casaus to 30 years. However, in 2018, the Court of Appeals overturned his most serious conviction; his failure to call for medical help for the dying boy, and his sentence was reduced to 12 years.

One of the reasons I've included Omaree's story here is that the recording of the telephone call to the police dispatcher (which you can find on Youtube; it makes for harrowing listening) gives us a clear snapshot of his and his siblings' life with their parents. Often we can only imagine the abuse the children endure. Technology such as this, along with text messages, which have been used in evidence in other cases, can give indisputable proof of abuse, but if ignored, as in this case, I feel that those responsible for doing so should be punished. The Officers' collusion with Omaree's parents, and advice to them to be careful what they say, lest it be misconstrued, is horrifying.

Omaree's life had been one of dramatic ups and downs. Born in prison to his crack cocaine-addicted mother, the little boy was fostered out to his aunt Sylvia's home at one year old, giving him the chance of a loving family. By the age of three, he was returned to his mother, only to be fostered by family friend, Essie Sotelo, between the ages of five and seven. With Synthia's consent, Essie and her family, including Omaree and his younger sister, lived for much of that time in Phoenix, Arizona, where he made friends and did well at school. Photographs of Omaree during this earlier part of his life show a much chubbier, healthier looking boy, who enjoyed playing football, eating pizza, and playing on his x-box. Despite this agreement, when Synthia Varela decided she wanted her children back, Mrs Sotelo found that her custody was not legally sanctioned by the courts, and, threatened with being charged with kidnapping, Essie reluctantly returned the children to their mother's 'care'. As we have seen many times, the children were taken from a safe and loving home, and handed back to their abusive parents; in this case, cocaine addicts who were not capable of caring for children.

According to the Albuquerque Journal, Synthia Varela and her sister Sylvia had a middle-class, even privileged, upbringing. Their father and stepmother both worked as Army technicians and their jobs took the family to Saudi Arabia, where they lived the ex-pat life; the children getting to see places other kids only saw in books. From their home base, they took many holidays, to places such as Switzerland, Italy, Jordan, Germany, Austria, Spain, Greece, Holland, Hawaii, Singapore and Hong Kong. But this advantaged start in life did not prevent Synthia from getting into trouble almost as soon as the family returned home to New Mexico, for offences such as shoplifting, prostitution, and drugs. By the age of eighteen, she was the mother of her first child and living with a drug dealer. Following a police raid on the home, including a shootout, the baby was removed and eventually adopted by Synthia's own parents. It is tragic to learn therefore, that Varela was known to the authorities, including the CYFD and the police, twenty years before Omaree's death at her hands. As is so often the case, if information had been taken seriously, shared between agencies, and acted upon appropriately, this little boy would have escaped his tortured life and death.

In the wake of his murder, a wrongful death lawsuit was filed by Omaree's estate against the Children, Youth and Families Department, accusing social workers of failing to exercise professional judgment and bungling their oversight, which increased the risk to the child's life. As a result, a settlement was paid to Omaree's three siblings.

The police department however, was not held to account in the same way. Four officers were 'disciplined', and another, Gil Vigil, was fired. The other officer who attended the home when Omaree made his call for help, Scott McMurrough, was suspended from his job for 56 hours. These 2 officers spent less than 15 minutes at the Varela residence, did not speak to any of the children, and did not make a report of the visit. The emergency operator seems to be the one person who realised the danger Omaree was in, and she begged the officers to respond and check the child, and file a report.

The Albuquerque Journal states that the APD also failed 'to properly respond to earlier calls of possible abuse, including when Omaree reported to school officials in 2012 that he'd been beaten at home by his mother'.

Drug abuse by caregivers is a significant factor in a high percentage of child torture/murders. As adults, we know to steer clear if an addict on the street is behaving in an unpredictable and violent manner. But their children cannot steer clear. They must stay in the family home and endure whatever treatment their caregiver subjects them to, whether as an everyday occurrence or as the result of a drug-crazed meltdown. In addition to the drug abuse, the Varela children were also prey to their violent stepfather, whose fluctuating moods, as recorded on the police dispatcher's tape, swung in a heartbeat between pure vitriol: "I hate you more than I hate anybody in my whole life," and demands that his show of affection be taken seriously: "We love you, we just want the best for you. Don't you understand that? I want the best for you. The best of everything."

Rest Safely in Peace, Omaree

Abdicating Responsibility

Synthia Varela is one of very few perpetrators who appeared to enjoy a privileged childhood, though of course we don't know all the facts. We do know that she turned to drugs in her late teens, and from that point on, lived a life of abuse and criminality, lacking responsibility for the care of her children.

There are addicted parents who are capable of giving their children all the love and care they need. But there are too many others whose minds are sufficiently altered to render them at best neglectful, and at worst, murderous.

If drug dealing could be reduced, on our streets, and in our schools and prisons, the lives of potential users and their children could be prevented from being utterly ruined. But of course, that is a huge task, well beyond the scope of this book.

Like Cheryle Butcher, mother of Daniel Valerio from the 2nd story in this book, Synthia Varela seems unable to take responsibility for her part in her son's murder.

And in my free book, *My Name is Isaiah Torres*, you will read that his father only accepts a small part of what he has done wrong, saying: "I abused my son, but I did not murder him."

Of the perpetrators in the stories I have published so far, abdication of responsibility for their child's death is a common factor. Some come closer than others in realising what they've done, but generally, the lack of self awareness is staggering, and if we were to study it, could perhaps be beneficial to those striving for prevention.

From Volume 3, Al Mutahan McLean describes his young son as a predatory paedophile, and in Volume 4, just three weeks after his death, Max's murderers turned the room in which they had imprisoned him for several years into a playroom for their other children.

Along with Angela McAnulty's words from Volume 1:

"I shouldn't have spanked my daughter with a belt," as if using the belt was her only misdemeanour, the lack of understanding of their crimes beggars belief.

And in the words of the sadistic great-aunt who murdered Victoria Climbié in the UK in 2000:

"I loved that little girl, she was my daughter in my heart."

Nobody's Child

'DEBRA! GET DOWN from that wall! I won't tell you again!'

'Sorry, Miss Scarff.'

'You're going to have to pull your socks up and behave yourself, my lady.'

'Yes, Miss Scarff.' Under my breath I'm chanting what the boys say. 'Scarff, Scarff, makes you wanna barf.' And anyway, my socks haven't fallen down. I keep them up with elastics.

Even my granny says Miss Scarff's loud and pushy. And that's saying something, because Granny isn't exactly the quietest person in the village.

The other dinner lady is much nicer than Miss Scarff. *She* says I'm too skinny and brings me biscuits. I daren't tell Granny though. She'd go mad that somebody was giving me food.

I'VE MADE A FRIEND at school. She started after the rest of us because she came 'from away'. It means she talks a bit different, but I like it. But she's not here today, so this dinner-time I hang around near some of the bigger girls who are sometimes nice to me. But they're just ignoring me right now. Big girls are like that. When they run away, I lean against the wall and watch the other kids in my class until the bell goes.

'Well, Debra! Are you going to come inside or are you going stand there and take root?'

It's okay. It's only Miss Brown, my teacher, and she's smiling.

'HI, DEBRA.'

Oh, that's good, my friend Lauren's back for afternoon lessons.

'Where've you been?'

'To the doctor's.'

I bet it's because she's so chubby, and the doctor thinks she should lose weight. When the nurse came to measure our height and weight last week, she said that I was too thin and Lauren was too fat. I'm going to ask her what she eats at home because I want to be more like her.

She starts to tell me a bit more, but Miss Brown has just come in, so she just grins at me instead.

Lauren and me are the slowest at learning to read. We're on the same book, and it's mostly pictures, but Lauren has to keep waiting for me to catch up. She's nice that way. Miss Brown tells us we're both doing well, and we are good girls to help each other. I sometimes wish Granny was as kind as Miss Brown.

Before Lauren came, I was the only one who still couldn't read any words at all. I don't know how everyone else had learned so quickly. But I heard Miss Brown say to Granny that I'd soon catch up because I was trying really hard. There's only thirty of us altogether. In the whole school. Anyway, Miss Brown said not to punish me for not reading yet; there's plenty of time. Granny does get cross with me for being slow though, and it's not very nice.

WHEN LAUREN COMES through the school gates the next morning she's trailing behind two older children, weighed down by their bags. They grab them off her and run into the school.

'Aren't they Miss Scarff's two kids?' I ask her.

She nods.

'Well, why were you carrying their bags?'

'Because they told me to. Come on, better not be late.' And she skips ahead of me into class.

After we've had our school dinner (shepherd's pie then apple crumble, mmm) and we're playing in the yard, I notice that Miss Scarff seems to be watching us. I mean, I know that's her job and everything, but she's supposed to watch the other kids too.

'I don't like Miss Scarff,' I say.

Lauren looks horrified. 'You can't say that!'

'Why not? I think she's nasty and bossy.'

'What if she heard you?'

I think about it. I wouldn't really care, but if it got back to Granny I'd probably be in big trouble. 'Well, I'll say it quietly then.' And I whisper, 'Miss Scarff is nasty and bossy.'

We both giggle behind our hands and I drag Lauren round the side of the building where Miss Scarff can't see us.

'I'm watching you.'

I can't believe she's followed us.

'Get back into the main playground.'

We skip back round the corner, pretending we were going to do that all along.

'I don't even know where you live,' I say to Lauren. 'I'm not allowed friends to my house, but maybe your mum lets you.'

'No, same here.'

'Is your mum nice?'

'She's okay. I don't live with her though. It's just me and Daddy and my gran.'

'I live with my granny too. Don't you miss your mum, though? I miss mine, but they took me away from her a long time ago because they said she wasn't taking good care of me.'

Lauren shrugs. 'My mummy took me on holiday to Turkey once.'

'Wow! Turkey. That's miles away.' I've never been further than Downham Market. 'Was it good?'

'It was hot.'

I stop myself just in time before I say that she probably felt extra hot because she's plump. That wouldn't be a nice thing to say. 'Was there waterslides?'

'Oh yes. There was lots of things like that.'

I'm jealous. I can't help it. 'I've been to London.' I haven't though. 'I saw Princess Diana.'

She's impressed. 'I loved her,' she says. 'I used to wish she was my mummy.'

'Oh, me too. But now she's dead we would be too sad.'

'I suppose so,' says Lauren. 'She's with the angels now.'

'She's an angel herself, most probably.'

'Most probably. Now she's gone I wish my granny Christine was my mummy.'

I laugh. 'You can't say that! She's your daddy's mummy!'

'I know, but she's kind to me. And when it's just me and her and Daddy it's nice.' She sighs. 'But since she got a new job she has to work really hard and I don't see her as much. I miss her.'

We start a game of hopscotch and Lauren suddenly stops. 'That's my daddy,' she says, grinning. She's about to go across to the school gate when the tall man begins talking to Miss Scarff. 'I'll see him later,' she says.

'I wonder why he's talking to her,' I say. 'I hope she won't be getting you into trouble with him.'

'Me too,' she says.

A FEW WEEKS LATER, Lauren tells me she's got a secret. 'I'm going to be a bridesmaid.'

I grab her hands and make her jump up and down with me. 'Who for?'

'Miss Scarff.'

I stop dead in my tracks. 'Miss Scarff? Oh, very funny. I thought you meant it for a minute, but you're just kidding.'

'No. I mean it. It's for Miss Scarff and ...'

Miss Brown appears. 'The bell's gone, girls. Time for class.'

We go in and take our seats. 'You can get into trouble for telling lies,' I hiss at my friend. If I said something like that my granny would not be at all happy. And when she starts on me it's really not very nice.

'Debra!' Miss Brown looks annoyed. 'Concentrate on your work, or I'm going to have to separate you two.'

I glare at Lauren. I'm not sure I'd mind being separated from her if she's going to tell fibs.

But she looks sad and I feel sorry straight away. I smile at her. She smiles back.

Feeling very grown up, I decide that if you're real friends you *will* have some ups and downs. I reach for her hand under the table. A few little white lies don't matter.

Lauren rushes away from school at the end of the day, so I don't get chance to ask her who she's really going to be a bridesmaid for. And it's Friday, so I'll have to wait ages until I find out. I've never been a bridesmaid but I think it'd be lovely. I've noticed Lauren has lost a bit of weight, so that explains it. Nobody wants to be a chubby bridesmaid.

IT POURS WITH RAIN all Saturday morning. But Granny still sends me to the shop. On the other side of the road, I spot Miss Scarff sheltering herself and her son under a huge yellow umbrella, while the daughter walks alongside with a pink one. I make myself invisible. A few steps behind comes another little girl, laid down with bags, and with her clothes so wet they're sticking to her. It's Lauren! I look from Miss Scarff and her kids to Lauren and back again. The daughter yells at Lauren to hurry up. She's carrying their shopping! I watch them until they reach their house and I see Lauren following them inside. I'll have to ask Granny what it's all about. She'll know.

GRANNY CAN'T STOP LAUGHING. 'You mean, you didn't know? And the two of you thicker than thieves!'

'Didn't know what, Gran?'

She hands me a Rolo. 'You know who Lauren's dad is, don't you? The big fella that's never out of the pub while there's beer in the pumps.'

Of course I know who she means.

'And haven't you seen him talking to Miss Scarff? They say he's never away from the school gates these days.'

Well, yes, I've seen them, but I didn't think anything of it. But the penny's starting to drop. 'Lauren's going to be a bridesmaid, Gran.'

'Is she now? Going to make an honest woman of the loud-mouthed bitch, is he?'

'But, Granny, I don't get it. Lauren was carrying their bags, like a servant.'

'Well now, what do you expect of that Scarff woman? Loves her own brats to death, can't bear anyone else's. You know that from the school playground.'

I don't know what to say. Poor Lauren. Fancy ending up with Scarff the Barf as her new mum.

ON MONDAY, I ask Lauren about being a bridesmaid but she doesn't seem as excited as she was.

'Me and Dad'll be moving in with Miss Scarff and her two children. And I'll have to call her Mum.'

I'm trying to rub a purplish mark off Lauren's arm. 'Won't come off,' I say.

She snatches her arm back. 'Just leave it, Debra.'

'Oh, sorry!' I say it sarcastically and immediately regret it. 'No, I mean it, Lauren. I am sorry. I keep saying and doing the wrong thing. I do it at home and my gran gets mad at me.'

'Does she hit you sometimes?'

'Not very often, but she shouts at me. A lot. She usually cuddles me afterwards though, so I don't mind it too much.'

Lauren gasps, as if remembering something.

'What is it?'

'Oh, it's nothing.'

'Come on.'

'Granny Christine used to cuddle me, but I don't see her very much so I hardly get cuddled at all now.'

I laugh. 'Don't tease me, Lauren.'

'No, I don't. I really don't.' She looks kind of stunned. Like she's realised something important.

I put my arms round her. 'There you are. You've been cuddled now.' I'm surprised how thin she feels. She always wears a few layers to school these days so I hadn't noticed. I want to say something but I don't know how.

THE WEDDING is in July at the local church and at least half the village turns out to watch. People are saying how lovely the bride looks, but I don't think they mean it. I hope she doesn't look our way because I think my granny is sniggering, and Scarff the Barf might take it out on me in the playground. I wave at Lauren and she waggles her fingers so I know she's seen me. She looks nice but sort of tired and her dress is hanging off her a bit. Maybe she'll pass it onto me afterwards because I think it would fit me better. I'm bigger than her now.

They have the reception in the pub, and when I walk past later I spot Lauren waiting outside.

'Lauren! What are you doing out here? You'll be missing all the sandwiches and cakes!'

'Oh, I don't mind, Debra. Anyway, I was waiting for you.'

'But you didn't know I was going to come past the pub!'

'Well, it's too noisy in there. Dad's getting drunk and Mum's getting mad at him, even though she's drunk too.'

'Oh heck,' I say, giggling.

Lauren doesn't laugh though.

I DON'T SEE LAUREN again during the school holidays. I knocked on their door once, but Miss Scarff told me Lauren wasn't well and I mustn't knock again. Granny said that sometimes it's best to keep away from families like that, but I miss Lauren. I don't really have anyone else to play with.

The week we go back to school is a scorcher, and Granny says I can wear one of my best summer dresses. I see Lauren coming round the corner and run to hug her. She doesn't smell too good.

'I've missed you, Lauren.'

'Me too.'

'Heck, Lauren, get that big jumper off. It's boiling hot!'

'No, it's okay. I feel a bit cold.'

She looks like she's sweating though.

'Come on then, let's see what book we're on this term.'

But Lauren seems to have forgotten what we've already learnt, and this time it's me racing ahead of her.

'Lauren! Why aren't you concentrating? We've done that word loads of times.'

She looks like she might drop off to sleep any minute.

I stand up and grab her arm. 'Go into the toilets and take those tights off. I think you're getting tired because you're absolutely sweltering.'

'No!' She gives a funny little yelp as if I've hurt her. 'No, Debra. I'm fine. It's just getting used to school again. You know, after the holidays.'

'Yeah, you're right. I couldn't get out of bed this morning. Granny was going up the wall.'

The teacher comes up to us. 'Are you girls alright?' She looks closely at Lauren. 'You look a bit peaky, sweetheart. Maybe you don't feel well? I think I should send you home.'

'No! No, I'm alright, I promise.'

'Well, I'll have a word with your step-mum when she comes in at dinner time.'

'Please don't, Miss. I'm alright. Please don't do that.'

I DON'T THINK it's very nice of Lauren to just ignore me. I've waved at her twice and she's looked away both times.

'Leave her alone,' says Granny. 'I think she's embarrassed.'

'What for?'

Lauren's family is sitting on a big checked blanket near the water and Lauren is a little distance away. I'm trying to see exactly what's on the blanket because it looks like it's heaped with food, and Granny and me only have a cheese sandwich each and an apple for afters.

Granny says money doesn't grow on trees, but I bet she'll give me £1.50 for an ice cream later.

It looks like they've got pork pies and scotch eggs and those bits of cheese and pineapple and tiny pickled onions on sticks. I love them. The dog is with them and they're feeding him sandwiches. Then Miss Scarff, sorry Mrs Wright, seems to be telling him to go and play with Lauren, but as he approaches her he begins to snarl, and Lauren starts to get up so she can get away from him.

'Don't. Move!'

I didn't think I would hear them from this distance, but Mrs Wright does have a very loud voice. Why doesn't she let Lauren move though? My friend looks scared but stays where she is as the dog circles her, barking.

My granny is shaking her head. 'What is that woman up to? Her daughter looks terrified.'

Granny knows Lauren isn't her real daughter but I don't say anything.

After a few minutes, I hear Mrs Wright call the dog. 'Good boy. Come here, come on. Here's a sausage roll for you.'

They're drinking lemonade. I love lemonade, but we've just got water. I think Lauren must've had her lunch earlier because there's nothing scattered around the grass she's sitting on. She looks in my direction for a second and I hope she can see my smile. Then Granny and me concentrate on our sandwiches and watch the water go by. When I look back, Mrs Wright is standing up and dragging Lauren up by her arm. Then she punches her in the face.

I gasp and turn to Granny but she's already on her feet and over there in a flash. 'What the hell do you think you're doing?'

'This,' says Mrs Wright, and punches Lauren again.

Granny turns to Lauren's Daddy who's just sitting there with a scotch egg in his hand. 'Is this how you let your wife treat your daughter?'

He shrugs. 'She's the boss.'

'Too right I am,' says Mrs Wright, her face about two inches from Granny's. 'So, what are you going to do about it?'

Granny suddenly looks smaller, and older, and unsure of herself. 'I'll be reporting you, lady,' she says, and storms back to me. 'Come on, Debra. Time for us to go.'

I scoff the last bite of my sandwich and we gather up our things.

Lauren hasn't made a sound.

I'VE NOTICED that Lauren wears the same clothes every day now, and I think she'll be glad of the polo neck jumper now it's nearly Christmas, but I'd have thought she might've put on a coat as well. I don't say anything though. Lauren gets upset if I do. I once saw a bruise at the very top of her neck and on her chin, and when I asked her about it she said she keeps bumping into things. I'm really really far ahead of her in my reading now too, so we don't sit together as much.

And ever since the day of the picnic, Granny's changed her tune. Instead of telling me to stay away from 'that family', she keeps encouraging me to stick by Lauren now. 'She's such a sweet kid, Debra,' she says.

'I know, Granny. But ...'

'But what?'

'Well, she's really scruffy and she smells.'

'Don't let that put you off, Deb. She needs her friends right now.'

'I suppose so. But she doesn't say much these days. She's so quiet.'

'Try to stay friends with her, sweetheart. It can be your good deed. Did you give her those crisps like I asked you to?'

'Yes, Gran. She wolfed them down and never even offered me one.'

'You can have a packet at teatime. I'll give you some cheese and crackers for you to give her tomorrow.'

I'm not happy about that. Granny doesn't fuss about me this much. But I'd best do as she tells me.

'**DEBRA BAINES**, what do you think you're doing!' Scarff the Barf has swooped down on us like a witch on a broomstick.

'I wasn't going to take it, Mum,' says Lauren, shoving the piece of cheese back into my hand. 'I promise.'

'You little liar. You're in for it when I get you home.'

I need to think quickly. 'She wasn't taking it off me, Miss Scarff. I was just showing her what Granny's packed for my lunch today.'

'That interfering old cow.' She's towering over me. 'Do you think I was born yesterday?' It looks like she's going to belt me. I relax a bit when I remember that she's not allowed to do that.

'I'm sorry, Miss Scarff, I mean Mrs Wright.'

'Get out of my sight. Lauren, you stay here.' Before I've gone two paces she thumps Lauren in the arm. Three times. She must be allowed to hit Lauren because she's her daughter now. I think that's a silly rule.

I DON'T SEE MUCH of Lauren anymore. She has lots of days off school and when she comes in she looks poorly. She used to have beautiful thick blonde hair but now it's wispy and greasy looking. And she's still in that same polo neck jumper! I try to get her to play chase with me in the playground but all she wants to do is sit down with her back resting against the art room wall. When I ask her what's up, she just smiles. A bit.

The other kids have started to whisper about her. They don't include me, so I'm not sure what they're saying. I'm just glad that none of them seem to pick on her. In fact, I've even seen Lauren's stepsister and brother being really nice to her; they gave her a Penguin biscuit once and a Breakaway another time. So they're not as bad as I thought they were.

GRANNY HAS FRIENDS round at our house, and even *they* seem to be talking about Lauren. The first time I heard her name, I thought I was making a mistake, but I wasn't.

'Well, I'm going to try again.'

'But they just don't seem to listen.'

'They've got to. Someone *has* to listen.'

'I don't know what's going to happen if they don't.'

'Something awful.'

'She told the doctor it was the dog that did it.'

'He wouldn't believe that though, surely.'

'What do *you* think? She's still there, isn't she?'

'It's a shame Christine's not around as much. She used to keep her eye on things.'

'And where's her dad in all this?'

'I think he just tries to keep the peace.'

'Well, he needs to step up. Can't he see how thin she is? She's like a stick insect.'

'Poor little mite.' It sounds like Granny is crying.

'Oh, Helen. Don't upset yourself.'

'We need to try again. I'd take her in myself if they'd let me.'

It goes quiet for a few moments.

'It happened to me,' says Granny. 'That's why me and my brother were taken into care. It's why our Ronnie's in such a state now.'

'Oh no, Helen. I'm so sorry. Is he inside again?'

'For dealing this time.' I hear Granny blow her nose. 'But we need to do something about Lauren. Before it's too late.'

'What more can we do, though?'

'I'll try social services again.'

'Listen, has anybody been to the police?'

'I have,' someone says.

'I told the doctor.'

'Why isn't the school doing anything?'

'Right,' says Granny. 'Let's all contact the authorities again. And we won't give up. They'll have to listen to us, and protect that little girl.'

I didn't see Lauren after that. And I really missed her.

An Overview of Lauren's Case

Lauren Wright

16.07.93 - 06.05.00

aged 6 years & 10 months

Norfolk, England

Lauren was born in Hertfordshire, England to Jennifer Bennett and Craig Wright. By all accounts, the couple's affair was short lived, with Wright requesting a paternity test to prove that he was Lauren's father. Later, in a bizarre bid to rid herself of her daughter, Jennifer Bennett abandoned Lauren at a Turkish airport following a family holiday, scratching Lauren's photograph out of her own passport. The British consulate had to organise the little girl's return, and Lauren was placed on the Hertfordshire 'at-risk' register. In Bennett's own words, 'I wasn't the best mother in the world'.

Lauren was later removed from the register, when Craig's mother, Christine Wright, who was concerned for her granddaughter's safety, was granted a residency order and became Lauren's legal guardian.

In early 1999, when she was five, Lauren went to live with her father and his mother in the village of Welney in Norfolk. Their next door neighbour was school playground supervisor, Tracey Scarff. Scarff had children of her own, a nine year old son, and a six year old daughter, whom she treated well, but once Craig Wright moved himself and his daughter in to co-habit with Scarff, Lauren became the butt of her violence and cruelty. Having escaped abuse in her birth mother's home, the little girl was placed in one where she would suffer even more.

Craig and Tracey soon married. Lauren's grandmother popped in regularly, but when she took on a demanding new job in January 2000, she had less involvement with her granddaughter, and Tracey's maltreatment of her stepdaughter increased in its frequency and cruelty.

Perhaps having become accustomed to a life of neglect with her birth mother, it seems the little girl did not complain to any of the adults around her that her stepmother was hurting her. And her father did not protect his daughter.

Having been a chubby child, as she was systematically starved over the seventeen months leading up to her death, Lauren's weight plummeted to two stone, and her blonde hair was falling out. Tracey Wright gave plausible reasons for the bruises that began to appear on Lauren's body, including being knocked over by the family's Alsatian dog, a wardrobe falling on her, a variety of childhood ailments, and walking into doors.

When the suspicions of concerned neighbours were reported anonymously to social services, a Child Protection enquiry was instigated. Lauren was examined by a doctor who did not believe that her injuries, including numerous bruises of various ages, were accidental, and referred her to a paediatrician. Tracey Wright claimed that Lauren was being bullied at school, and although teaching staff said this was not likely, the paediatrician was convinced by Wright's excuses, and Lauren was not removed from the family home.

We see this time and again in child murder cases; a perpetrator presents a convincing case to various agencies, and the child is left in the abusive home. This is why I feel my ABCD mantra is so important:

Assume Nothing
Be Vigilant
Check Everything
Do Something

We should not assume the perpetrator is telling the truth, much as we may want to.

Concerned neighbours and teachers noticed that Lauren was losing weight, looked listless, and was almost always dressed in shabby long-sleeved tops along with tights, whatever the weather. They correctly suspected it was to hide the numerous injuries on her body, in addition to the bruising they could see on her face. They said Lauren used to walk behind the rest of the family, sometimes carrying their bags, and unprotected against bad weather.

Along with the beatings Lauren was subjected to, witnesses later testified that she had been made to stand inches from a gas fire, was punished because she had wet the bed, and was forced to eat revolting food, such as soup with a worm dropped into it and sandwiches smothered with pepper. It was also said that Mrs Wright encouraged her own children to hit Lauren.

We find these deliberate acts of torture hard to understand. But they don't spring from nowhere; they build up over time, perhaps beginning with a slap or harsh words.

Social workers from Hertfordshire, the county of her birth, visited Lauren at home on 25 April 2000, to discuss a matter in connection with her birth family. Shocked by Lauren's appearance, they wrote to Norfolk social services (where she now lived) expressing their concerns. In fact, in the last twelve weeks of her life, Lauren was seen several times by social services and medical professionals, but the evidence of abuse was not urgently responded to, and the decision to remove Lauren to safety was not taken.

Further calls were made by anxious villagers, who could not believe that Lauren was still being left at home to suffer, and social services arranged to visit the family on 8 May 2000, which was 2 days after she died. Perhaps that visit would have saved her life.

During the first week of May, Lauren was reported to be off sick from school due to gastroenteritis. On 6 May, Christine Wright was alarmed when her daughter-in-law shouted for her to come and help with Lauren, who was motionless on the bed. In desperation, Christine attempted to give her granddaughter mouth-to-mouth resuscitation, but it was in vain. Lauren had been killed by a blow to the stomach that collapsed her digestive system. She was covered in at least 60 bruises from top to toe, including several on her shins caused by kicks, or blows with an object.

People from the village were astonished to witness Tracey and Craig Wright visiting the pub soon after Lauren died; the latter being rather subdued, whereas Tracey Wright was seen to be laughing and joking.

At the trial at Norwich Crown Court, Tracey Wright's son gave evidence that he had seen his mother punching Lauren twice in the belly; possibly the fatal blows.

Tracey Wright was sentenced to fifteen years for manslaughter and wilful neglect, and Craig Wright was sentenced to three years for the same crime, although there was no evidence that he had actively played a part in Lauren's death.

During her time on remand, Tracey Wright had boiling water thrown over her by other prisoners, and it seemed likely that she would serve her sentence in solitary confinement for her own protection.

The serious case review that investigated Lauren's torture and death was critical of the fact that no multi-agency case conference was ever called to discuss the child's situation, despite a number of agencies separately believing that she was being abused. Norfolk social services admitted that their handling of Lauren's case was negligent, saying that if they had followed the correct procedures they believed that Lauren would still be alive. Those who missed vital opportunities to save Lauren are struggling to live with their mistakes, and various improvements have been made to child protection procedures in the wake of the review. I admire their honesty; not all agencies are willing to acknowledge that errors were made. And the finding that if a multi-agency conference had taken place, Lauren might well have lived, seems to be a simple enough course of action for others to take in future cases of child abuse and neglect.

There are 2 points here which are not uncommon in the cases I write about in this series. Firstly, that other children in the family may be treated 'normally', whilst one, often but not exclusively the youngest and / or a stepchild, is singled out for abuse.

Secondly, in this Volume alone, we see several children taken from one abusive environment to another. Lauren was treated shamefully by her birth mother and subsequently by Tracey Scarff. Christian Choate was taken from a situation of suspected incest and abuse at his birth mother's home, to be placed in a cage and tortured to death by his father and stepmother.

It is unbearable to contemplate that some children are mere pawns to their caregivers, and that even if they do find a place of safety, such as Lauren did with her paternal grandmother, they can be snatched away and thrown into the lion's den.

Rest Safely in Peace, Lauren

The Unwanted Child

Lauren's mother abandoned her at a foreign airport. Her father asked for a paternity test and later witnessed her abuse. Was Lauren created through nothing more than an inconvenient by-product of sex?

If sex education begins early enough for teenagers to know that having sex can produce a baby, and if we make contraception easily available, we work towards fewer unwanted babies, although mothers do slip through the net and bring unplanned babies into the world.

Whilst illegal in most countries, in France, a woman can give birth legally and safely in hospital, and leave her baby there. Other countries, including Pakistan, Italy and Germany, have their own systems of keeping newborn babies safe.

Amid a certain degree of controversy, Baby Boxes are set up in various countries and several US states, where a new mother can leave a baby she cannot care for in a specially designed 'box' set into the wall of a hospital, church, fire station, etc. The first scheme, Door Of Hope, installed its first box in South Africa in 1999, with the aim of saving the lives of babies who would otherwise have been abandoned or abused, and may have died.

After discovering that she had been abandoned as baby, Monica Kelsey set up Safe Haven Baby Boxes in the US, and she works to educate others on the Safe Haven Law. She offers a 24-hour crisis line, counselling, and refers some women to adoption centres, and some to crisis pregnancy centres.

Being Prepared For Parenthood

Whilst, in the UK, midwives and health visitors often provide support throughout pregnancy and for up to five years after the birth, some parents do not fully engage with these services and babies can go unseen and mothers unsupported.

In addition, many countries are unable to fund a comprehensive service, and even in the relatively well-off UK, cuts to public spending pose a threat to the safety of babies and toddlers. However, these health workers are in a unique position to prepare the parent(s) for the difficulties that babies can bring, and to raise concerns where appropriate. Midwives and health visitors can repeatedly stress that babies don't cry just to annoy their parents, and that their natural bodily functions are not under their babies' control, and will improve with patience and encouragement.

From 'Flour Babies' – a bag of flour that some UK ten-year-olds keep with them at all times, over a three week period, arranging a baby-sitter if they need to go somewhere without their charge, to trials throughout the world, using the RealCare Baby 3 infant simulator, with teenage girls given a lifelike doll to care for, youngsters are exposed to some of the realities of being responsible for a 'baby'. The jury is still out on the success of these well-intentioned schemes.

The Good Student

IT MUST BE A GOOD PARTY because my uncle and aunt are shaking their heads and tutting. Us kids are running riot but Mom doesn't seem to mind. She likes to see us having fun, and there wasn't a lot of that in the refugee camp. The party's for the latest group of Somalis to arrive here safely, and I can already tell that this is going to be a better life for us.

Mom doesn't know many people, but her friend Yazmin should be here somewhere. She's nice. She was the first person to welcome us here to New York State. Is it really only two weeks ago? Yazmin's told Mom that her cousin is coming tonight, and she's really looking forward to meeting her. With any luck she'll be as nice as Yazmin, and hopefully Mom will make another new friend. She needs to get out and get to know people so she can settle in here. It's easier for us kids. Just give us a football and a piece of waste ground and we're off.

'Time for us to go,' says my uncle.

'I think I'll stay,' says Mom. 'Is that okay?'

My uncle looks at my aunt, and then nods. 'That's fine, Shukri. Let the kids enjoy themselves. It's about time they had some fun.'

My stern uncle telling us to enjoy ourselves! To have fun! Wow, things really are different here!

'Thanks, Brother,' says Mom. 'I'll see you next week. Oh, don't go yet. Here's Yazmin at last.'

It's easy to see how fond of each other Mom and her friend have become. Yazmin's been a really big help; finding us a place to live, helping Mom get us kids into school, and getting Mom a cleaning job working alongside her. I don't think it's easy for Mom without a husband, and we all miss our dad. But Yazmin has been the next best thing.

Everybody hugs each other and Yazmin introduces the tall, black-skinned man at her side. 'This is Ali Mohamud, my cousin.'

Ah, so this is the cousin.

Mom holds out her hand. I can see she's trying to hide her disappointment but it's all over her face; I mean, she can hardly go shopping or share cooking tips with this one. My uncle looks more like his usual self, and by that I mean, annoyed; a man who isn't family shaking his sister's hand. The Somali culture hasn't quite disappeared then. But my uncle will have to adapt. We're all having to find a good balance between the old and the new.

'See you, Brother, Sister,' says Mom, practically throwing them out of the door of the community centre.

'I'm starving,' says Yazmin, putting her arm around Mom's shoulders. 'Where's the food?'

'Oh, there's tons of it,' I say, leading the way to the trestle tables.

'Of course there is!' says Yazmin. 'Come on, Abdi, serve us something nice.'

I scoop up the cous-cous, spilling a little on the cloth. 'There you go, Yazmin. Would you like some, Mr Mohamud?'

'No, thank you. Maybe later.'

It's not long till the call to prayer sounds and the men head off to the mosque a few houses away. Us kids don't have to go.

I can hear Yazmin whispering to my mom. 'So ... what do you think of Ali?'

'Huh? Well, he seems okay.'

Yazmin laughs. 'He's a bit serious, isn't he? He's been in the States a while, but just recently moved to Buffalo, so I don't actually know him that well. Not bad looking though, is he?'

I glance up at Mom, who's blushing.

'Aha!' laughs Yazmin. 'I'd better tell my cousin to watch out!'

'Don't be silly, Yaz.'

Mom's eyes are starting to glisten.

'Hey, hey,' says Yazmin. 'Why the tears?'

'It's the relief. We've made it here. Sometimes I thought we never would.'

'I know, I was the same. But you *are* here. And you and the kids are finally safe.'

Mom nods and wipes her eyes with her scarf. 'I feel they could do anything.'

'So many opportunities for them here.'

'It's fantastic for them. But look at the little ones running around like wild things. I'm going to let them tear about all weekend; spoil them like crazy. Then on Monday it's business as usual. Abdi, go ahead and have fun. You don't have to stay beside me.'

'I'm okay, Mom. I've beaten them all at table tennis anyway.'

'Go on, son. We can clear up here.'

I still hang around though.

Mom turns back to Yazmin. 'Mind you, I don't want their grades to slip. They were all doing so well back home, even with everything going on.'

'I bet they'll be fine. Not like my two. I think they're allergic to homework. I don't know how you manage with yours!'

'I want them all to get good jobs. Like my oldest Ahmed has; I'm so proud of him.'

Yazmin digs Mom in the ribs. 'I hadn't noticed.'

'Their dad was clever. Actually I think Abdi's the one who takes after him the most.'

My ears prick up.

'But their dad wouldn't have cared what their grades were as long as they were happy. Mind you, I don't want Abdi winding up cleaning offices like me!'

'ALI LIKES YOU.'

Mom and Yazmin are side by side, dusting the office desks. I'm tagging along with them today; doing my homework amid their sprays and buckets.

'Don't start that, Yaz,' says Mom. 'Anyway, he's stern; he reminds me too much of my brother.'

'He's a much nicer person on the inside.'

'Hmm, I'll take your word for it!'

'You did say he was good-looking.'

'No, it was you who said that! Anyway, big difference between that and being a good person. I'm not ready, Yaz. Not even for getting to know him better.' She looks over at me, and I put my nose into my English book.

'Don't blame me if he gets snapped up then, Shukri.'

'I won't. Anyway, how come he's not married already?'

'He has been. Got kids, didn't I mention that?'

'Uhm no, you didn't.'

'Honestly though, Shukri. Don't be too slow; he really does seem to be one of the good ones.'

'Maybe.'

'Hey, anyway, how's the kids?' says Yazmin. 'This one seems to be doing okay.'

We grin at each other. Yep, I like Yazmin. I've got a great friend in her son, Mehmet, too.

'The rest of them settling in at school alright?'

'Yeah, not too bad. Though sometimes they seem more interested in their X-boxes and watching cartoons than their lessons. And that includes you, Abdi!'

'Aww Mom, don't forget I was top of the class last week.'

'Wow, Abdi, well done! That's great, Shukri. Especially when he's had so much change going on.'

'I know, I know. I'm proud of him.' Mom reaches across and ruffles my hair. 'I'm proud of them all. And I'm glad I've got Ahmed for most of the little jobs my husband would've done.'

'I help too, don't I, Mom?'

'Yes, Abdi. You do. Frightened of being left out for a minute, son?'

I laugh. 'Well, who fixed the fridge door?'

'Yeah, you're right. But neither of you have managed to sort that dripping tap.'

'You see, Shukri,' says Yazmin.

'See what? Oh okay, I guess some things are harder without a man!'

Yazmin starts to drag her vacuum cleaner into the next office. 'Funny you should say that; I've got this good looking cousin …'

I pick up my books to follow them. They're right, I don't like to miss anything!

'IS YOUR MOM at home? Yaz says you've got a faulty tap.'

It's Yazmin's cousin, Mr Mohamud. He takes up all the room in the doorway.

'Mom! Mom, there's someone to see you.'

Mom pushes her hair under her scarf as she comes through. 'Oh, hi Ali.'

He holds up a wrench. 'Tap need fixing?'

'Yes, yes it does.'

'Well, that's what I'm here for.'

'Okay, yeah that'd be great. Come in. Would you like a drink?'

'Tea, two sugars.'

'Abdi, would you make Mr Mohamud a cup of tea?'

'Sure, Mom.'

'Settling in okay, Shukri?'

'Yes, I like it here. How about you? Yazmin says you haven't been in Buffalo very long.'

'It's okay, I guess. Some things are very different to back home. But I like being so close to Canada. I always wanted to go there as a kid.'

I gasp and slop tea over the rim.

'Well, you've got a friend right there,' says Mom. 'Abdi's always talking about the Rockies and the Mounties and all that, aren't you, son?'

I nod as I put the mug down in front of Mr Mohamud. I hang around, hoping he'll talk more about Canada.

Mom smiles. 'Sometimes life gets in the way of the things you want to do though, doesn't it?'

'You've got that right, Shukri. Hey, maybe I could take you there one day. Have a break from your job and the kids. It's really not that far.'

Mom looks shocked, and I'm sure Mr Mohamud blushes. It's hard to tell.

'Just for a drive, y'know.'

I can see Mom's uncomfortable. 'That sounds nice. But the kids ...'

'We could take them.'

That's more like it.

'Hmm, yes,' says Mom. 'Sounds good.'

I HAVE NO IDEA how it happened. I know that Mom *should* be married, but it all moved on so quickly. Dad (I have to call Mr Mohamud 'Dad' now) and his kids have joined us, and it's been tricky for Mom, trying to manage all six of us, and carrying on doing her cleaning job. The kids are pretty nice though. The house is crowded but we all get along. Dad works every hour he can at the newspaper office. As a security guard, he works nights, so he's around when we get home from school and Mom's gone out to work. He's taken on the job of making sure we do our homework. It's never been any trouble to me though. I love school and learning new stuff.

'How're you getting on with that Geography assignment?'

'Yeah great, Dad. I'm just gonna start writing about the Great Lakes.'

'Which one are you starting with?'

'Erie, I think.'

'Good choice, son. Leave it on the table, and I'll have a read of it when I get back from work.'

'I might not have finished it by then, Dad. Mehmet said he was gonna come round and play some games. I don't have to hand it in till Thursday.'

'Do the work first, Abdi. I'm looking forward to reading it.'

There's a knock on the door.

'I'll get it on my way out,' says Dad. 'Oh hi, Mehmet. No, I'm sorry, he can't. Not tonight. He's busy with homework.'

I wonder whether to jump up and argue with my dad, but think better of it. I'll ask Mom. She'll let me have a break.

MOM, DAD AND I are walking down Hoyt Street towards the International School. I know us kids are supposed to dread parents' night, but I'm looking forward to it. I'm an A student. Well okay, with the odd B thrown in there, but I know Mom and Dad are going to be proud of me. The gym has been cleared, and the teachers are all sitting at desks around the outside of the room. Kids and parents are jostling for position in the queues. Finally we get to the desk and sit down in front of Miss Poole. She's a great teacher. She's a kind of hero to me. So clever and patient.

'Well, Abdi. I think you know what I'm going to say.'

I sure hope I do.

'He's doing very well, Mr and Mrs Mohamud. One of my class stars.'

I sneak a look at Mom's face.

'We're really proud of him,' she says.

'You should be. All A's, with the occasional B. We couldn't ask for more.'

My dad is listening so intently it's like he's hearing it for the first time, even though he reads my report card practically every day. 'Oh, I don't know, I think we *could* ask for a little more.'

The moment's awkwardness is broken by the appearance of the principal, Mrs Jamil. 'He's an excellent student,' she smiles at us. 'Keep it up, Abdi. We're expecting great things of you.'

'So are we,' says Dad.

We catch Yazmin and Mehmet on the way out. They look pretty pleased with themselves too.

'He's gone up to a B average,' says Yazmin. 'And that's in spite of all the football and video games! We're going for ice-cream to celebrate. Want to come along?'

Mom's smiling and nodding and looks ready to say 'Yes', but Dad cuts across her.

'No, Yazmin. I'm sorry,' he says. 'Abdi and I need to get back home and work on those B's.'

At first I think he's joking, but he grabs my hand and leads me away. 'But, Dad.'

'Not now, son. Let's get home and talk.'

DAD'S DECIDED it's better for me to do my homework down in the basement where there's no distractions. It's not bad, as basements go. There's a few old toys down there, some of Dad's tools, a sink in the corner. And of course the desk and chair that Dad carried down for me. He usually sits in an old armchair and reads the newspaper while I get my head down into my books.

'Abdi, are you concentrating?'

I must've been staring into space again. 'Yes, Dad. I'm concentrating.'

'Carry on, then. I shouldn't have to tell you.'

'Sorry, Dad.'

'Okay, I'm going to get ready for work. Make sure you finish that History project and the last two pages in your Math book. Leave them out for me to check when I get back home.'

'Okay, Dad.'

That's a heck of a lot of work, and I feel tired. When I hear the door bang I go up the stairs so I can watch cartoons with Ahmed for a while. I can go back to my books when I've had a break.

'Abdi!' says Ahmed. 'Dad's still here ...'

I turn round. My dad is standing in the doorway. I don't know who can have slammed the front door.

'Sorry, Dad. I just need about a ten minute break.'

'No, Abdi. No breaks. History's one of your 'B' subjects. You need to get that grade up.'

I know there's no point in arguing. 'Okay, Dad. Sorry.'

He follows me back down, and when I turn to look at him he has a strange expression on his face. 'I'm sorry, Abdi. It's for your own good.'

The rolling pin meets my shoulder and I leap backwards. 'Dad, what are you doing?'

He whacks me again. This time on my face, though thankfully, not quite as hard.

'Dad, stop. I don't understand.'

'Stay down here and do your work. Don't go to bed until you've finished.' He turns on his heel and goes up the steps.

I sit there, stunned, for a long time, then open my book. Dad's under a lot of pressure; his job's stressful, and we're quite a big family. It can't be easy.

'YOU'RE QUIET, ABDI.' Mom is washing the breakfast dishes and I'm drying.

'I'm okay, Mom.'

'You sure?'

I nod.

'What's all this fighting I've been hearing about? You've still got a black eye.'

'I told you, Mom. It was nothing. Just a bit of shoving on the school bus.'

'It's not like you to get into a fight.'

I shuffle my feet and mutter. 'I do sometimes, Mom. Anyway, I told you. I hit my head on the bar.'

'And the other boys haven't been bullying you?'

'No, Mom. Just leave it. Please.'

'Well, don't forget to pick up your lunch box for school. I don't know how you forgot it yesterday.'

'Sorry, Mom.'

But I set off without it and Mom has to follow me down the street. 'I don't know what's the matter with you these days, Abdi! I have enough to think about with the little ones.'

'I know, Mom. I'm sorry.' I hesitate. 'Mom, do you think I could stay with Auntie for a while?'

'Oh, son. Why?' She tries to hug me close, making my shoulders damp with soap suds, but I keep my arms stiff at my sides. 'I would miss my big, clever boy too much.'

'You could come and see me every day. Auburn Avenue isn't far away.'

She crouches awkwardly beside me. 'But son, why do you want to go there?'

I look all around. Everywhere but at Mom.

'Abdi, why?'

My eyes start to water. 'It's nothing, Mom. Don't worry. I'll see you tonight.' And I shuffle away, my bag of books dragging down my right hand side.

MY BROTHER AHMED is calling down the basement stairs. 'Mehmet's here for you.'

I start to tell him to send Mehmet away, but I've done all my homework, and I can come back in an hour and do all the extra stuff Dad's been giving me. 'Okay, I'm coming.'

'Dad's doing one of those weird shifts, Abdi. So I'm not sure what time he'll be back.'

'I'll just have a little kick around with the guys.'

'Don't be too long. But I'll cover for you if I have to,' says Ahmed.

'Thanks, Bro .'

It's a nice evening and it feels fantastic to run about with my friends.

'You've still got it, Abdi,' says Mehmet. 'But how about giving the rest of us chance to score?'

I feel like I'm flying when I leap up and head the ball between the two piles of sweaters. 'Another goal for the unstoppable Abdifatah Mohamud!'

Mehmet high-fives me. 'Who's coming to my house for sodas?'

I look at my watch. 'Not me; I'd better go. See you guys at school tomorrow.'

Dad is on the front doorstep when I get home. 'Where have you been?'

'I've been to Mehmet's, Dad. We've been doing our homework together.'

'So where are your books, son?'

'We just used Mem's books, Dad ...'

'Don't lie to me, son.' He pushes me into the kitchen, slapping at my head and kicking my legs.

'Dad, please stop.'

'Don't you tell me to stop.' He suddenly grabs me by the neck, and squeezes.

I try to make him let go but I can't breathe. My ears start buzzing and my eyes won't focus.

'You *will* do as I tell you,' he screams into my face. He's reaching for something on the kitchen counter with his free hand. His machete. He was using it earlier to split a coconut. It's just out of his grasp; I need to make sure he doesn't reach it.

His fingers close round a heavy metal serving spoon instead, and he starts to beat me, on my arms, my shoulders and my back.

I've found my voice and I'm yelling and screaming, but I know the others can't hear me. I can hear the TV blaring in the living room. When I fall to the floor, he kicks me in the stomach.

'Help! Ahmed, help me!'

Finally, he stops. 'Wait there, I haven't finished with you. I'm going to fucking kill you one of these days!' He's going upstairs.

I vomit into the sink, and a trickle of blood wets my upper lip as I grab the phone and dial 911. The operator asks me some questions and then says they'll send someone. I can hear Dad moving around in the bedrooms. If only Mom was home. I wonder if I should run to my auntie and uncle's house. Or even just go in and tell Ahmed. My legs are shaking and I feel dizzy. The police are taking forever. I call them again. 'Please, please hurry. He's going to kill me.'

They arrive just as Dad's coming back down the stairs.

'I believe there's been some trouble here tonight.'

Dad tells them we had an argument because I wouldn't do my homework. 'Isn't that right, son?'

I know this is my chance, but I hesitate when I see the look in Dad's eyes.

'Come on, lad,' says one of the officers. 'What's the problem here?'

I clear my throat. 'Dad hurt me. He was trying to choke me, and he threatened me with this.' I reach for the machete.

'That's some weapon there, Mr Mohamud.'

Dad laughs. 'I was just joking around.'

'Did your Dad cut you with this, Abdi?'

I have to tell the truth. 'No, he didn't. But he ...'

'There's a small cut on his lip,' says the officer.

'Bit yourself by accident, didn't you, Abdi?' says Dad. 'Those can be really painful. I'll have a look at it in a minute.'

The officer puts his hands on his hips. 'Well, I can't see any bruises on the boy.'

Under my t-shirt, look under my t-shirt! And there must be finger marks on my neck.

'It's like I said,' says Dad. 'You wouldn't do your homework, would you, son?'

I daren't say anything else, so I hear myself saying, 'Yeah, that's right.'

How can I tell them any more while Dad's standing right there?

Anyway, Dad seems calmer. Perhaps it'll be okay when they've gone. It's the first time he's really hurt me. He won't do it again.

'**MOM,**' I SAY, as I catch a bit of TV with her after Dad's gone to work. 'I don't want to stay home every night doing homework. I never get to play football anymore.'

'Oh, Abdi, come on. You know we want you to do well at school. You could grow up and do anything you want. Dad thinks you could even be a scientist or a doctor. Imagine that!'

'But I *am* doing well at school. My grades are still high. So can't I play football too?'

Mom sighs. I know she's had a hard day with the little one's cough. 'Oh Abdi, not now.'

'Please, Mom. I'm losing all my friends. They say I'm a book-worm. That I'm just no fun anymore.'

She pushes the hair out of her eyes with the back of her arm. 'Okay, okay. I'll see what I can do.'

'Thanks, Mom.'

'I love you, Abdi. You know that, don't you?'

'Course I do, Mom.'

'And I'm so proud of you. So's Dad.'

'Yeah, I guess.'

DAD LOCKS US BOTH in the basement now when he makes me study. When he leads me down the steps my legs turn to jelly, because I know he'll find a reason to punish me. Last week he filled the sink and put my head under the water because I couldn't remember the capital city of Scotland. He held me under as I spluttered and fought for breath. When he pulled me back up by my hair he asked me again.

'Glasgow,' I whispered.

'Idiot,' he said, and pushed my head down again.

THE FIRST TIME he bound my legs to the chair, I screamed.

He punched me. 'Shut up you cry-baby. Do you want Ahmed to hear you?' He brought his face down to mine. 'Well, do you? Because if you tell anyone, I'll kill you.' He said it so calmly. And I almost believed him.

But today he's forgotten to lock the door behind us. He's prowling around, slapping that rolling pin into the palm of his hand. He'll ask me my multiplication tables later, and I know I won't be able to recite them. I've learnt and learnt them but they fly out of my head when Dad stands in front of me, his head bent down so we're almost nose to nose, that furious look in his eyes.

'Get on with your History while I read the paper.'

My eyes keep going in and out of focus. It looks like Dad's tired too. He sometimes falls asleep over the newspaper. When he starts to nod I usually reach down to the check the bindings on my legs. Just in case. This time they don't seem too tight. I push my finger down under each of the neckties. If he falls asleep I can get them off, I know it. His head flops down onto his chest. I work furiously at the knot at the back of my left calf. I've made it slacker but I can't untie it.

Dad grunts and I freeze. Wait a minute or two. I feel for the knot on my right leg. It's much looser and falls apart in my hand. Back to the left one.

Dad's head lifts up and he mutters, 'You working hard, Abdi?'

'Yes, Dad,' I whisper.

His head drops again. As the left tie falls to the floor, I watch him. His chest rises and falls in a steady rhythm. His breath comes slower and deeper.

Without giving myself any more time to think, I creep away from my desk and up the stairs. My heart is pounding. I'll go to Auntie and Uncle's or maybe to Mehmet's house.

I sneak out of the front door and start to run.

The traffic's busy on Sycamore. I glance at my watch but it's hard to read while I'm running. I guess it's rush hour. The streets seem longer than when I'm walking or running along them just for fun. At last, I've made it as far as Jefferson and if I can just get over this fence, I'll be home free. I'll go and see Mom at work tomorrow and tell her everything. She won't make me go back. She'll bring my clothes and my X-box round to Auntie's. And Dad won't mess with my uncle. Heck, this fence is tricky.

My heart sinks like lead when a woman pulls up in her car. I recognise her from the neighbourhood. I grapple with the fence but my hands won't grip the top and I can't pull myself up. I glance behind me and confirm what I feared; Dad's in the car with the woman. Before I can run again, he gets out and reaches up to grab my hand. The woman follows him.

'I want to go to Auburn Avenue,' I whisper to her. 'Just let me go there. I'm going to see family. I'll be okay.'

I think Dad must've heard me, because he looks at his watch with his free hand, then scratches his chin as if he's considering it. 'No, come with me now, Abdi. Everything's going to be okay.'

I don't look at him. 'I don't want to go with him.'

'Come home, and we'll wait for your mother,' the woman is saying.

Dad tightens his grip on my hand.

What can I do?

'Just come and sit in the car so we can talk,' says the woman.

I'm still clinging to the fence. 'I don't want to. Please, don't make me.'

'Nobody's making you do anything. It's just, you can't be running around the streets like this. Look at the traffic, you could get hurt.'

'I want to go to Auburn. To Auntie's house.'

'Maybe you could go there tomorrow,' says Dad.

'Doesn't that sound okay?' says the woman. 'Sort things out at home and take it from there?'

With a sinking feeling, I let them help me down. 'Can I sit in the front with you, then?'

She nods, and Dad climbs in the back.

'Your dad says you had a little falling out over your homework. He's told me he's not going to hurt you.'

I close my eyes and breathe deeply. 'He always says that.'

'Okay, so why don't I take you both home, and when your mom gets home you can all have a talk about it.'

I swallow hard, and nod.

As the woman drops us off at home, she says I must get in touch with her tomorrow if things aren't okay. I shrug my shoulders.

As soon as she's gone, Dad drags me down to the basement and dunks my head into the basin of filthy water.

He yanks my head up, and I splutter. 'No, Dad. No! You said you wouldn't!'

He shoves my head down again, bashing it against the hard white sink. I gulp in air and water when he pulls my head up again by my hair.

'Help! Dad, please stop!'

But he's dragging me towards the chair and tying my legs to it. And the neckties are nowhere to be seen; it's duct tape this time.

'That's too tight, Dad! Oh please, don't do this!'

'You lazy, ignorant fool!' he yells at me. 'If you can't do as you're told, I have to make you obey me!'

'Please, Dad! Please, stop!' I scream at him, desperately hoping he'll come to his senses.

But he unrolls more duct tape, and as I struggle against him, I tell myself that the lady in the car, and my mom, and the teachers, and the police and everybody will help me tomorrow. But this time Dad binds my arms as well, and when I keep trying to protest, he shoves my school sock into my mouth and wraps more duct tape round it. My eyes and nose are running; I can't breathe.

Why, why, why did I come back with him?

I thrash back and forth, side to side.

Help me, someone.

He's picking up the rolling pin.

Oh please, somebody help me.

An Overview of Abdi's Case

Abdifatah Mohamud

17.09.01 - 17.04.12

aged 10 years & 7 months

Buffalo, New York State, USA

Abdifatah was his mother's pride and joy; a bright, hard-working boy who loved playing video games, and watching cartoons with his brothers and sisters. Gentle, though lively and full of fun, he studied hard at school, with ambitions to do well and get a good job.

Abdi's mother, Shukri Bile, had not had it easy. Fleeing the genocide in Somalia that killed her first husband, she finally found refuge in a camp in Uganda, where Abdi was born. When she arrived in Buffalo, she was optimistic about the future for herself and her children.

Just two weeks after her arrival, Shukri met and later married Ali-Mohamed Mohamud, who had also arrived from Somalia two years earlier. They had six children between them.

But Ali-Mohamed Mohamud was a strict parent, who checked the children's homework every night, and felt that Abdi's grades were slipping. Ironically, teachers at Abdi's school said this was not the case. Headteacher, Kathy Jamil, testified that the fifth grader was doing well in school, always achieving A's and B's. Other members of staff who knew Abdi said he was a good student and punctual with his homework assignments. He had won awards for his essays and been top of his class. The promising young student had described his teacher, Miss Poole, as 'his hero'. Tragically, Abdi had once told his teachers that he would 'be killed' if he did not do well in a test.

In an attempt to get protection from his stepfather, Abdi had previously rung the police on at least two occasions. He had done so in early April 2011, a year before his murder, ringing back soon after to ask them to hurry. The officers reported that they did not see any evidence of abuse, although they admitted that they did not ask the boy to remove his clothes in order to check for bruising. Abdi told the officers that his stepfather had choked him and threatened him with a machete. Mohamud's response to Abdi's claims of abuse was that they had had a disagreement about his homework. When Child Protection Services further investigated the complaint, Abdi must have been too frightened to proceed, as he withdrew the allegation, and the little boy was not removed from the home for his safety.

Just two months later, in June of the same year, Abdi came to school with bruising and two black eyes, and the authorities were called. CPS were again involved, but Abdi told them that he had not been beaten by his stepfather and had instead been part of a fight on the school bus. The other children supported Abdi's story.

At 5pm on Tuesday 17 April 2012, a woman driving her car down Sycamore Street in Buffalo, NY state, spotted a young boy running as fast as he could along the sidewalk. A few moments later, she saw a man running down the other side of the street, trying to cross the busy road. The woman turned her car around and stopped to help the man, letting him into her car. The man told her the boy was his son and he didn't want anything to happen to him. When they found him on Jefferson, trying to jump over a fence, the man got out of the car and took hold of his hand. The boy said he didn't want to go home with his stepfather and was trying to get to a family member's house on Auburn Avenue. But he was coerced into the car and sat in the front with the woman driver, who told him, 'Daddy promises nothing is going to happen.'

The boy replied, 'No, he always says that.'

As she dropped them off at their home on Guilford Street at 5.20pm, the woman told the boy. 'You go home, and if something does happen, you let me know tomorrow morning.'

But Abdifatah could not do that. Because when they entered the house, his stepfather forced him into the basement, tied him to a chair with duct tape and electrical cord, stuffed a sock into his mouth and, covering it with more duct tape, he beat him at least seventy times with a large rolling pin. When the boy vomited, he took the time to replace the sock, and then resumed the horrific assault, crushing the back of Abdi's head and exposing his brain; separating the ten year old child's head from his spinal cord.

The woman who gave Abdi and his stepfather a lift home was a neighbour of the family, with young children of her own. She said later, 'I may well have been the last person to see that little boy alive.' I'm sure she lives with dreadful guilt. But unless Abdi was obviously physically hurt, do we know how we ourselves would have reacted? Because most of us *still* can't quite believe that a child is going to be murdered by their parents.

Immediately after he had brutally murdered his stepson, Ali Mohamud, who worked as a security man at The Buffalo News, rang his supervisor and asked if they could meet at their workplace. When the two men met at 11pm, Mohamud told his supervisor that he had come to clear his locker, saying, 'I have a lot of problems and killed one of my kids.'

The police were called to the office building, and Ali Mohamud stood up calmly to be arrested and handcuffed. He then accompanied the officers to the police station, where he gave a statement admitting that he had been involved in the death of his son. Mohamud claimed that he was trying to discipline Abdifatah, because they had got into a fight over his homework and Abdi was kicking him. Mohamud stated that it was the first time he had ever been violent to his stepson, but the previous police visits to the home told a different story.

In the meantime, when Abdi's mother could not find her son that evening, she called the police, and Officer Christopher Fields searched the house, finding Abdi's body in the basement, covered by a blanket.

In October 2012, Mohamud was put on trial for his stepson's murder, with Erie County District Attorney Frank Sedita III calling the crime one of the worst he had seen in 24 years as a prosecutor. Chief Medical Examiner Dianne R. Vertes testified that the slightly built ten-year-old would have been alive for much of the savage beating, and that she had also found evidence that Abdi had been almost drowned, and that he had ligature marks on his neck, and a knife wound on his arm.

The jury took less than three hours to return their verdict, with prosecutor Thomas M. Finnerty saying, "Justice has been done". At his sentencing, Ali-Mohamed Mohamud seemed to be seeking forgiveness, with the words, "If only I knew what I was doing that fateful day; I never harmed anyone before."

Buffalo Police Department launched their own investigation into their handling of Abdi's calls for help, whilst also saying that they had reported the allegations to Erie County Child Protective Services. It seems that the latter did not do enough to protect Abdi by removing him to a place of safety.

Mohamud was convicted of second degree murder and sentenced to twenty five years to life in prison for the murder of this kind-hearted and clever boy, who'd had a promising future ahead of him.

Rest Safely in Peace, Abdifatah

Violent Discipline

Ali-Mohamud clearly felt justified in 'disciplining' Abdi to force him work ever harder on his school-work.

Synthia Varela seemed nonplussed that her form of 'discipline' eventually killed her son, saying: 'I kicked him the wrong way', implying that there is 'right way' to kick your child.

I cover this more fully in Volume 1, but it bears repeating that if a parent never begins using physical discipline, then it can't escalate to violent discipline, where perpetrators often use the excuse of punishment gone wrong.

It would be of enormous benefit if those caregivers who defend physical chastisement would join the campaign to end it completely, opening their minds to the fact that in some cases 'mild' physical discipline sets the foundation for increasingly violent abuse.

Some of these defenders are responsible and loving parents who never administer more than a light swat, and feel it is an effective punishment, particularly if given as a warning to a child who is on the verge of doing something dangerous. I do understand that. But we need to ask all adults to remember those children who are not blessed with reasonable caregivers who know when to stop.

It is my dream that those parents would relinquish this form of control (because their use of it makes it seem acceptable) and choose another, for the sake of the thousands of children whose parents do not use smacking 'responsibly', and instead, discipline their children to death.

Some pro-spankers claim that it is ridiculous to compare them to these 'monsters'. But the monsters once also administered spankings 'for the good of the child'.

I intend to explore more fully the parts of society where whole groups of adults actively encourage physical punishment for the slightest infringement of their rules, strongly defending their right to deliver 'spankings' of varying severity, as part of the accepted culture of 'training up' their child.

I believe that if we stop physically disciplining children, the cycle of abuse within the family will be broken, and abusing children to death will be on the path to eradication.

Supershock

'WILL YOU FREAKING WELL sit down, Ethan!' I know I'm yelling again but the kid drives me crazy. He takes no notice, of course. He's been trying to stand up in the trolley ever since we came in. Yeah, he's a bit big for it, but it's the only way I can get round the store without him tearing up and down the aisles. I turn to my friend. 'I don't know how you get PJ to behave himself.'

She laughs. 'Yeah, he's a good boy'. She nods at her toddler sitting quietly in the trolley.

I run my hand through my hair. 'I'll have Family Services round again if I'm not careful,' I say. 'I'll go nuts if they take him off me again. Ethan, sit the fuck down, NOW!'

Tracy nudges me. 'Calm down, hon. Hey, let's go to McDonald's after this.'

'With him? Are you freaking kidding me?'

'How about the park, then? We can let these two have a good run about.'

I hesitate. I haven't really got time. But it's tempting. 'Yeah, okay then.'

My Ethan's a little older than PJ, and as I expected, he's soon darting all over the place, with his friend toddling along behind. My son spots the duck pond and makes straight for it.

'Ethan! Come back here. Right now. He'll be in there in a minute, Tracy. I'd better get him.' The small heels on my shoes aren't good for running on grass but I manage to catch up to them and grab Ethan. 'My God, Ethan. What do you think you're doing?' I turn and start to walk back towards Tracy. 'Follow me, PJ. See! Do you see, Ethan? PJ does what he's told. Why can't you?'

My boy puts out his tongue and I react instantly and slap his face. He looks stunned for a second and then it starts. The wailing. 'You want something to cry about, Ethan? Do you?' I don't even know how many times I slap him, but Tracy is soon upon us and wrestling him off me.

'Hey, hey Diane. That's enough now.'

'Oh my God, what am I doing?'

'It's okay. Come and sit down. PJ, get the pack of M&M's from the bag, and you and Ethan can share it.'

PJ looks confused but does as Tracy asks.

'Now, what's all this about?'

I'm snivelling like a kid by now. 'It just comes over me, Trace. I can't help it.'

'You were scared for him, hon. You didn't mean to slap him.'

I look at her gratefully. 'I was terrified he was gonna get in the pond and drown.'

'See, that's all there is to it. You don't have to get all upset about it.'

'I'm trying so hard. But I do get mad.'

'We all do, honey.'

'Not you, Tracy. You're amazing with PJ. Even though he's not yours.'

'It's not always perfect, Di. He can be naughty at times.'

'Yeah, I guess they all can. Oh, I really do love Ethan.' I look over at my son; he's giggling and tucking into those M&M's. 'I'm sorry I shouted at you, baby. I'm sorry I slapped you.'

'S'okay, Mommy.'

'Give me a cuddle?'

He gets up and toddles across to me. 'It's okay, Mommy. Don't be sad.'

I don't deserve him. I really don't.

PJ has followed Ethan, and is holding the bag of candy out to me.

'Oh, thank you, sweetheart. Now, which colours should I have?'

'Make pee-pee,' says Ethan, and I can't help but sigh.

'I'll take him, Di,' says Tracy. 'We'll go to those bushes over there. I'll race you, Ethan.'

As they start running and laughing, I feel PJ's little hand in mine.

'Auntie Di,' he says.

'Yes, baby?'

'Auntie Di kind to me.'

'Oh, sweetheart, you're easy to be kind to. Come give me a hug.'

THE NEXT TIME we go shopping, Ethan's pretty well behaved, but I can sense Tracy's still concerned about me.

'McDonalds this time, Diane?'

'I'm not sure, Tracy.'

'Well, back to mine then. I'll make something for us all. C'mon, you know you want to!'

'I don't know. If I'm not back for Abe getting home ...'

'Abe, Schmabe! Doesn't he let you do your own thing?'

I know Patrick gives her lots of freedom. He's good looking too. I'm so jealous of her I want to scream. 'How'd you manage it, Tracy? Well behaved kid, good man. All that shit.'

She shrugs. 'Just comes natural, I guess.' She sees my face. 'I'm kidding, Diane. I know it's hard. Really hard. Doesn't Abe help you out?'

'Him? You wouldn't even think it was his damn kid. All he ever does is tell Ethan to quiet down when he's watching the game.'

'Patrick does that too, babe. They're all the same.'

'But doesn't Patrick do all sorts of shit with PJ? Bathing him and everything?'

'Yeah, I guess so. But listen, Di. You gotta get a hold of that temper. Cos if you carry on, Family Services *will* start thinking about taking him away again.'

'Sometimes I wish they *would* take him, Tracy. I could hurt him, y'know. I don't want to, but sometimes I could really swat him, just like last time.'

'Come to my place, Diane. We can talk it out, okay?'

Tracy's trailer is a few down from mine, and the layout's the same, but she keeps it a whole lot cleaner. Sure, it's not shiny-clean, but there's not quite as much dirt on her floors, or empty cans to wade through.

Patrick's home watching TV when we struggle in. 'How's he been?' he asks. 'Anything you need me to take care of, honey? Oh hey, hi Diane.'

'No, it's all good,' says Tracy. 'Diane and me are just gonna grab a beer and catch up.'

'You girls have fun. I'll mind the kids for a while. Come here, PJ.'

The little boy toddles over and stands before his father.

'You been good for your mama?'

'Yes, Poppa.'

I hadn't noticed before how quiet PJ's voice is.

'You sure 'bout that? No fussing or crying or saying how you're hurting here, and here?' Patrick taps his son's head and arm.

PJ flinches slightly. 'No, Poppa.'

'You two girls go ahead and sit outside in the shade. I'll deal with what needs dealing with.'

'He's been good and quiet, I promise you, honey.'

'I said I'd deal with it, hon. Off you go now, girls. Hey, don't forget your beers.'

'It's just with us having company, y'know. Any dealing can wait.'

'I know, baby. It's fine.'

Tracy grabs two beers and a bag of chips and heads for the door.

'You got a good one there,' I say when we're settled in the tiny front yard.

'I guess I do. But hey, we came here to talk about you. You getting to the end of your rope again?'

I sigh. 'Feels that way sometimes. Sometimes I wish I'd never even had a kid.'

'You mean that, Diane?'

'I think I do. Not always, but hell it's hard work. Ethan really pushes my buttons. Knows exactly how to do it. It's like he does stuff just to spite me.'

'Oh Di, I'm sure he doesn't.'

'It feels that way sometimes. And I've got Abe's mom checking up on me all the time.'

'Try and think of it like she's looking out for you. Making sure you don't snap again.'

'Yeah, I'll try. She's a nosy old bat, though!'

Tracy laughs. 'It was only two lousy bruises, Diane. Hasn't everybody done that some time?'

'Yeah, maybe. But last week, in the park, I could've really lost it again, y'know.'

'I know.'

'Anyway, how d'you get PJ to be so good?'

'He's always been good, I guess. That first day I met Patrick he had PJ in his buggy. I remember it was snowing, and PJ fussed a little. But one look from his dad and I never heard another sound.'

'I just wish I could control Ethan without spanking him. That's what got me into trouble. I spank too hard.'

Tracy shrugs. 'Kids need discipline, Diane.'

'A little, I guess. But Abe's mom saw me do it. I'm sure it was her called Family Services.'

'Then maybe do it when nobody's watching. Warn them they're gonna get it when you get them home. That way you can keep them in line but nobody can poke their nose in.'

'But the bruises, Tracy.'

'Don't worry. Some kids bruise easy. Didn't he deserve that spanking anyway?'

'Well, he *had* been messing me around all day.'

'Look, don't feel bad about it. You just did what we all do.'

I nod, almost convinced, and lounge back in the chair.

After the beer, I stand up, suddenly needing the bathroom. Through the window into the trailer I see Ethan standing in the corner, facing the wall. PJ is on his back, over his father's knee, with Patrick's head bent over him. From where I'm looking, I can't tell if Patrick's giving his son tummy kisses or biting him. I turn away and say loudly, 'I guess I'll just go and use the bathroom.' When I glance back again, PJ is sitting up on his poppa's knee, and Ethan is staring at them both, looking confused.

I look pointedly at my watch. 'I guess it's time we should run along home now, Tracy. I can use my own bathroom.' I gulp down the last of my beer. 'Thanks for the talk.'

'WE DON'T SEEM to have seen PJ for a real long while, Tracy. He doing okay?'

'He's okay, I guess. But he's starting behaving so bad lately, and Patrick's had to keep him inside a lot. Y'know, to punish him.'

'That quiet little kid? He always seems so good.'

'Oh, you don't know what he's like, Di. I didn't like to complain with you having all that trouble with Ethan, but I swear that kid does stuff just to make us crazy.'

'Aww, well Ethan misses him. We'd sure welcome him around our place some time.'

'Yeah, I'll see what Patrick says. But with PJ not being my kid, y'know, I don't make the rules.'

A FEW DAYS LATER, Tracy turns up at my trailer door with PJ in her arms.

'Hey, Tracy. Hey, PJ. Come on in. I'm sorry, but Ethan's taking a nap right now. I just got him to settle.' My trailer's a mess. Ethan's toys are everywhere and the sink's full of dirty dishes.

'That's okay. I just came to say Hi to you, hon.' Tracy picks her way through the chaos, and flops PJ onto the sofa. 'Got any cigs, Diane?'

'Didn't I tell you? I gave up.'

'Oh, Jesus. Okay, I'll go back and get mine. PJ, don't move from that sofa. Make sure he doesn't move, Diane. He's still being punished.'

'Oh, okay.' As the door bangs behind her I go to give PJ a cuddle. But he goes as stiff as a stick and starts to tremble; it's as if I've electrocuted him. 'Hey PJ, it's me, Auntie Diane. I'm not gonna hurt you none, baby.' As I look closer, I see some oval-shaped marks on his neck.

Surely they can't be fingerprints. He stares at me in terror as I lift up his tiny t-shirt and realise what's different about him. He's skin and bone. But more than that, his little body is criss-crossed with the unmistakable imprint, as deep as an orthodontist's impression, of teeth marks.

'Auntie Di,' he says in his tiny voice.

'Yes, sweetheart?'

He starts to cry and I gently hold him.

'Auntie Di.'

'Who hurt you, baby?'

'Not tell.'

'You can tell me, baby.' I hug him closer.

He buries his head in my breast and is really sobbing now.

'Come on, baby. Hey, it's okay.'

The door is opening and I sit PJ up and pull his t-shirt back into place. Something tells me not to say anything to Tracy just yet.

'I thought I told you not to move!'

PJ still has hold of my hand as he cringes away from Tracy.

'You been crying?' Tracy glares at her stepson. 'What you been crying for?'

'No, Tracy. Don't be cross with him. His eyes just got a little red there when he was rubbing them.'

'Not been talking or nothing?'

'Heck no, Tracy. You've been so quick.' My mind is racing. Do I tell her what I've seen? I need to think. What's the best way to help PJ? 'We didn't have time to do more than just look at each other, and notice how pretty we both are. Ain't that right, PJ?'

Tracy seems to settle down again, as I frantically try to think what to do, what to say.

'He said he needs the toilet, Trace. I'll just take him.' Before she can stop me I lift PJ up and carry him to the bathroom. All I want to do is cuddle him, but PJ tries to scramble out of my arms.

'Drink.'

'Sure, baby. Auntie Di's got some real nice lemonade for a good boy like you.'

'No, drink. Drink now.' He seems to be trying to lift the lid on the toilet. 'Thirsty.'

'Okay, sweetheart.' I run the cold tap and fill Ethan's plastic cup. PJ grabs it out of my hand and gulps it down. 'More. Please, more.'

'What you doing in there?' calls Tracy.

PJ freezes.

'Let's go back, PJ. Let's get that lemonade.'

Tracy is flicking through a magazine.

'The little guy seems kinda nervy, Trace. Is everything okay?'

She laughs. 'Yeah, sure. Why?'

'Oh, nothing. Hey, I'll just go and get us all a drink of lemonade.'

'Not for PJ,' says Tracy. 'He'll wet the bed tonight.'

'But he said … oh never mind. Come on, PJ, sit beside me.' I need to feel his little hand in mine.

I can't think straight, and Tracy's started jabbering about her own birth kids over in Lewistown, and how she's going to get to see them soon.

It's a relief when Ethan wakes from his nap and starts to cry.

Tracy jumps up. 'PJ's not allowed to play with Ethan. Like I said, he's being punished. I'd better go.'

'Hey, maybe he could stay here with me? Just for a bit.'

PJ's grip on my hand tightens.

'No, Diane. He's not allowed to play with Ethan.'

'I just thought I could give you a break.'

'PJ, come on. We're going. Your dad said we couldn't stay long.'

PJ looks back at me as she drags him out, and I long to take him in my arms.

Okay, okay, what should I do? I cradle Ethan and kiss the top of his head. What's going on with PJ? I know I should call Family Services, but they know me, for chrissakes. What if they start looking up close at me again?

Ethan smiles at me, then I put him on the floor so he can play with his train. It seems such a long time since that day I lost it with him. Even the time at the duck pond feels like ages ago. I still pray to God that seeing his mommy lash out at him won't scar him for life. I guess I'm like so many girls on the trailer park. Now that Abe's working away again, most days there's no man around to help out, and things get on top of me sometimes. I sure could use a man right now. Or just anyone to ask what I should do. About PJ, I mean. Somebody is biting that kid, and those were man-size teeth marks. But why? There has to be an easy explanation. But I can't think of any reason right now that isn't plain and simple cruelty.

I look down at my son. 'Remember the last time we went to PJ's trailer after we'd been shopping?'

Ethan grins. 'You *girls* sat outside with a beer!'

'You got that right. And when we were outside, did you and PJ have fun in the trailer?'

His ears are starting to turn red. 'Sure, Mommy.'

'Was there something going on with PJ and his dad?'

Ethan shrugs. 'PJ's dad is weird sometimes.'

'How, Ethan?'

'Huh?' He's running his toy train along the floor, between my legs. 'You make a good bridge, Mommy!'

'I do?' I try to snatch a cuddle but he's too involved in his game. 'Ethan, let's talk a little. Come on.'

He makes like he's ignoring me, but I know he's listening.

'It looked pretty weird in there that day. With PJ and his dad.'

'Yep, sure was.'

'You seen anything like that before, son?'

He's still looking away, but his ears are burning red. 'Some.'

'You mean sometimes? You've seen PJ's dad go weird on him some other time?'

'A bunch of times.'

I don't want to upset my little boy, but I need to know what's going on. 'How, son? How have you seen his dad go weird?'

'Apart from the biting? And beating on him?'

I steady my breathing. 'Come sit with me, Ethan. Please. Mommy needs a cuddle.'

He leaves his train and clambers up onto my lap.

'Does he beat him like Mommy did to you one time?'

Ethan shrugs. 'About ten times harder. PJ gets hurt real bad.'

I'm starting to feel sick. 'He does? What does Mr Bourgeois use to beat on him with?'

'His belt. And his hands too. He makes a fist like this and pounds PJ all over. PJ cries and screams, and his daddy tells him to shut up.' Ethan's eyes have filled with tears. 'Mommy, is it okay to tell you? I don't want to get PJ into any more trouble.'

'Yes, it's okay. He won't get into any more trouble.' I squeeze him tight. 'Can you tell me what happens after the beating, baby?'

'Well, one time I heard his daddy say he was gonna tie him up tight so he couldn't move his arms or legs, and he didn't care how much he was hurting.'

I swallow hard. 'Did you see Mr Bourgeois tie PJ up? How does he do that, Ethan?'

My boy hesitates before nodding. 'He puts sticky tape around his arms and legs. He makes it real tight too. Don't tell PJ's daddy I told you, will you, Mommy? He told me not to tell.'

'I won't tell him, Ethan. But I need to know what happens when PJ gets tied up?'

'Well, I guess his daddy shouts real loud and beats on PJ some more. He says he's gonna leave him like that all night so he can't move or get up to drink from the toilet.' He cocks his head. 'Why does PJ do that, Mommy?'

I have to think quickly. 'I guess his daddy leaves a cup of water in the bathroom. You know, in case PJ gets thirsty during the night.'

'No, Mom. He drinks the water out of the toilet. Not from a cup. That's gross, isn't it, Mommy?'

'There'll be a good reason, even if we can't think of it right now.'

'I don't think PJ's a naughty boy. Do you, Mommy?'

'No, I don't think he is either.'

'So why is he being hurt?'

'I don't know, Ethan.' I've heard enough; I need to do something. 'Listen, sweetheart, you mustn't worry about him.'

'I'll try, Mommy.'

'I'm going to sort it all out, baby. PJ won't get hurt anymore.' I'll call Family Services first thing tomorrow.

'And PJ's daddy won't know that I told, Mommy? I don't want him to hurt me if he finds out.'

'No, he won't know. You've done great, son. Don't worry about it now, will you?'

'I won't, Mommy. But can you hug me one more time?'

I WAKE AT 2AM and wonder what in the hell's going on. I can hear bang, bang, banging on somebody's trailer door.

'Let us in, we're here to help you.'

More banging.

'Open up, ma'am, sir.'

My mind immediately jumps to PJ, and I know something terrible has happened.

Ethan stumbles out of his bedroom. 'What's that noise, Mom?'

'I don't know yet, son.' I peep between my curtains. There's at least two fire trucks and the guys are pounding like crazy on the door of Patrick and Tracy's trailer. Half the trailer park is awake by now and some are gathering outside, amid the barking dogs and flashing lights.

At last the door is opened and the firefighters squeeze in. Not much later, a tiny person is brought out and blue-lighted towards the hospital. Shaking, I let the curtain drop back into place and draw my son towards me. When they call on me, I'll be sure to tell them everything I know. But for now, all I can do is hold onto Ethan and pray that PJ's going to be okay.

An Overview of PJ's Case

Patrick Michael Bourgeois
(known as PJ)
18.09.92 - 28.02.96
aged 3 years & 5 months
Columbus, Ohio

Tracy Lynn Bratton must have panicked when she realised that her boyfriend's son was dying. After she called the emergency services, she and Patrick got busy. As firefighters hammered on the door of their trailer, Bourgeois and Bratton yelled at each other as they tried to remove all incriminating evidence that showed they had harmed the child. Putting their own needs way ahead of the toddler whose life might have been saved if they'd let the emergency services in, they wiped the surfaces clean as the firefighters battered on the door. But then, putting their own needs first was what they'd done all PJ's life.

No one but Bourgeois and Bratton knows what the little boy endured during his three years on earth, because they never had to stand in front of a jury and tell a court what they'd done. What we do know of his last day, we know from statements made to journalists by the people who tried to save PJ's life.

When Mike Bates and his colleagues from the Columbus Fire Department finally gained entry to the trailer, they saw a small child with deep bite marks all over his body, fingernail grooves on his ears as if he had been pulled around by them, and tape residue on his wrists and ankles where he had been bound after a beating, so that he wouldn't be able to move and help himself.

PJ was rushed to the Columbus Children's Hospital, where Paramedic Mike Cogdill was part of the team that tried to revive him: "Whoever had done this to him had tortured him to death ... Had they shot him in the head, he would have suffered less. They made sure that his death was slow and agonising."

Dr. Patrick M. Fardal performed PJ's autopsy, referring to the abrasions on the child's ears, cuts to his forehead and mouth, and 'abundant' blood coming out of PJ's nose. He also reported on the deep human bite marks spotted by the emergency team, and eight bruises on the underside of the skin of PJ's scalp, caused by hard blows to the head, which had the caused swelling and bleeding of his brain.

Dr Fardal found blood in the child's airways, lungs, oesophagus, stomach and small bowel. He summarised PJ's tortured death in a few words. "He was beaten and he was physically restrained, and while he was restrained he swallowed his own blood and choked to death on it."

Both suspects claimed ignorance of what had happened to PJ, but displayed an uncanny ability, each time they were then confronted with an incontrovertible fact, to find an explanation for each action they had supposedly forgotten about.

Bourgeois' first claim was that when his son wouldn't eat his eggs, he was sent to bed for the night, and in the morning he was dead. When questioned about the bite marks, Bourgeois' explanation was that PJ had tried to bite his finger, and so he had bitten him back. When asked about his son's other injuries, the father suddenly remembered that they had had a little tiff, and that he had backhanded the three-year-old. Later, he was asked how PJ might've choked on his own blood, and Bourgeois admitted that they had taped his ankles together and his wrists behind his back and left him in his bedroom; this seemingly being a regular punishment for the little boy. When officers searched the rubbish bin, they found the tape that the killers had hastily thrown away. They also found blood splatters on the bottoms of kitchen cupboards that they had missed during their frantic clean-up operation while the fire officers were battering at their door.

PJ's father, Patrick Bourgeois and his girlfriend, Tracy Lynn Bratton pleaded guilty to involuntary manslaughter, thereby avoiding a trial, and were sentenced to 7 to 25 years in prison. Therefore, no witnesses were called, the murderers didn't have to face the prosecutors, nor did they have to explain to a jury why their little boy had been beaten and left to die. As part of the agreement to plead guilty to involuntary manslaughter, the perpetrators asked for the option of 'supershock probation' to be included.

'Supershock' was introduced for short sentences of less than 90 days duration, giving a judge the option of freeing a prisoner early, at any time during their sentence, without a parole board hearing. The logic behind this was that the shock of being incarcerated would have been enough to ensure that they would not commit further crimes, and they should be allowed to complete their sentence under probation, outside of prison. Supershock was not intended for crimes calling for medium to long sentences, such as the killing of another human being.

Assistant Prosecutor Ed Morgan says that he agreed not to object to the incredible concession of supershock, because he believed it could never happen; that no judge would grant this to PJ's killers; the torturers and murderers of a three year old child.

However, three years into their sentences, long before their eligibility for a parole hearing came up, the two murderers requested supershock.

Once again, no witness testimony was permitted on the day the court convened to decide whether Bratton could be released at this early date. But someone who desperately wanted her voice to be heard, on behalf of PJ and all those who had tried to save his life, was Linda Manley, an emergency nurse who was present when PJ was admitted to the hospital. She wrote a letter to the judge, confirming the nature and extent of PJ's wounds, but Franklin County Common Pleas Court Judge Nodine Miller would not allow Linda Manley to speak, as she was not the victim. PJ was the victim, and he was dead; he could not speak. But no one was permitted to speak on his behalf.

The judge described the child's death as a 'dramatic event' which 'was fraught with ignorance, immaturity and inexperience, more than malevolence'.

Astoundingly, in a statement that turns logic on its head, she also said that "these particular circumstances were so aberrant, it is hard to conceive of such a replay in the killers' lifetime." Therefore, PJ's murderers were *released because the crime they had committed was so heinous*. Additionally, Judge Miller recommended that Bratton should be set free in order to care for her own two children. (Up to this point, Bratton's children had been cared for in Pennsylvania by a family member who had now become unwell.) Yes, you did read that correctly; a child torturer and murderer was being released early in order to care for children.

I have included PJ's story in this collection, not only to honour his short life, but to demonstrate how proceedings can massively favour the fate of the criminals instead of their victims, subverting justice, and to show the gulf between the sentences different murderers serve. For example, Jeanette Maples' mother (from Volume 1) is on death row. Bratton and Bourgeois are free.

On 25 October, PJ's case became the subject of an Oprah Winfrey show. Amongst the viewers of the show who were saddened by the fact that PJ's grave had just a metal marker instead of a headstone, were citizens of PJ's birthplace, Lewistown, Pennsylvania. They proceeded to band together to raise $7000 in three weeks, so that the little boy could be afforded the dignity of a headstone and a dedication service. Linda Manley, one of the nurses who had tried to save PJ when he was brought into the Emergency Room, and who had unsuccessfully tried to be a voice for PJ at the supershock hearing, was one of the people who spoke at the service in honour of PJ.

I include here the letter that Linda Manley was not permitted to read out at Bratton's hearing:

Dear Judge Miller

I am here today to adamantly oppose shock parole for Tracy Bratton. ... As an emergency nurse, I was present during [P.J.'s attempted] resuscitation on Feb. 28, 1996. In my almost 25 years of experience, nothing prepared me for what I saw that day. [P.J.'s] entire body was covered with bruises, abrasions and bite marks; in addition, ligature marks were found on his wrists and ankles, indicating he had been bound for a long period of time and struggled to breathe. [He] was tortured to death.

[His] heinous death struck a chord with me and my colleagues. We followed his case closely through the criminal justice system, and we were quickly initiated into the confusing array of sentencing laws and practices. The [killers] were convicted of involuntary manslaughter, not murder, due to the difficulty of proving 'intent.' [P.J.'s] death was justified as a misadventure in discipline ... 'poor parenting'.

I find this explanation ludicrous and insulting. Parents do not punch, beat, bite and tie up a three year old child simply because [the child] will not eat [his] lunch. This is called torture. ...

Early release of Tracy Bratton denigrates [P.J.'s] memory. ... Justice equates to Tracy Bratton serving every second of the [original prison sentence]. A small child is dead because of [Bratton's] wanton acts of cruelty. ...

In the aftermath of [P.J.'s] murder, I have tried to take positive action to ensure other children will not meet a similar fate. Their fate is now in your hands. I trust you will make the right decision: Deny parole."

When I'm researching cases, words often fail me, whether at the cruelty of the perpetrators who claim to have loved the child, or when they say they were just disciplining them, etc. And to tell these stories, I have to find the words somehow. But when a judge behaves in such an abhorrent way and shows no respect for the child who was tortured to death, there are no words, there are only tears of sadness and frustration.

Thank you to Cindy from Ohio
for alerting me to PJ's story

Rest Safely in Peace, Patrick Michael (PJ)

Blaming The Child

PJ was failed after his death by the ultimate 'authority', the justice system, and I find the judge's ruling to free his murderers unacceptable. Sadly, many other authorities and statutory bodies fail children time and again.

In staggeringly back-to-front part of the supershock release order, Judge Miller states that PJ was a difficult child whom Bratton could not control, and that he began misbehaving on 27 February 1996. We only have his murderers' statement that he was a difficult child. Once again, Miller decided to take their word for it. Remember, there had been no trial, no witnesses were allowed to speak; only the murderers were given a voice. And the implication here is that his alleged naughty behaviour was a reason to torture and murder him.

Furthermore, the examples given of the three year old child's 'misbehaviour' are heart-breaking. One such example is that PJ used to get up in the middle of the night to drink water from the toilet bowl. Anyone with a shred of common sense and compassion would've known that nobody is going drink from the toilet unless they are not allowed sufficient to drink and are desperately trying to quench their thirst, perhaps in an effort to stay alive. Another example of bad behaviour the murderers gave was that PJ wilfully banged his head against the floor. Rather conveniently, this also serves as an attempt to explain away the wounds on his head, although Dr Fardal said the wounds could not have been self inflicted in this way. And even if they had been, head banging is an accepted manifestation of extreme stress, but incredibly, the judge classed it instead as bad behaviour.

No one ever corroborated the story the killers gave. Miller based her decision on nothing but the word of the perpetrators of the crime, and Bourgeois and Bratton were both freed less than four years into their sentences. How fortunate they were to have Judge Nodine Miller dispensing 'justice' for their crime of torturing a three-year-old to death.

PJ's is the last story in this collection, and I hope you have found them all interesting and informative to read, without being too distressing (although I understand if you do, as I find it upsetting to write them).

Many people ask me how I am able to research and write on such a sad subject.

A few years ago, after a traumatic event, I came within half an hour of bleeding to death. During my recovery, I decided that I wanted to do something more meaningful with my life. Discovering how many children were being tortured in their own homes, I cried so much for those children, and couldn't eat or sleep.

So I started writing down how I felt, and I wrote my first story. Learning of more and more cases, I wrote more and more stories, until I had enough for my first book. Now I can't stop writing. But I wish there were no stories to tell.

Please don't feel bad for reading, and even 'enjoying' my books. You're facing up to what so many turn away from, and we need to be aware of the suffering that's happening right now, if we are to have any chance of protecting children.

> If you've been moved by the children's stories and would like to help me raise awareness, a **star rating or review** for this book enables new readers to find my books.

This book is dedicated to the memory of

Charmaine, Daniel, Christian, Ayesha, Omaree, Lauren, Abdi, and PJ

Help To Protect Children ...

Please review in your usual way, or the QR code or link will help you to get back to the book's page:

https://mybook.to/Abused-To-Death-2

Then scroll waaay down
until you see Write a Review
(usually on the left side)

> Reviews help to spread awareness of abuse.
> Just a star rating or a few words is enough.

If you prefer, there are direct 'Easy Review Codes' at the back of this book, which take you where you need to be.

Your Next Book in the Series

Are you ready for more stories like these?

Volume 3 covers six more cases, including the story of **Takoda Collins**; imprisoned in his father's attic for years, and forced to hold torture positions for up to 20 hours each day. Surveillance cameras alerted his so-called caregivers if Takoda moved a muscle, when they would subject him to further hideous cruelty, including violating him with a wooden chair leg, and tasering him using an electric dog collar.

Find your copy in your usual way or:

Just scan this code:

Or **use this link**:
<u>https://mybook.to/Abused-To-Death-3</u>

Join Us On Facebook

After I'd built up a following, with discussions and photos, to honour the murdered children …

Facebook suspended my Page without explanation.

And everything is gone.

So please **Follow Me** and help me to start again!

Just scan this code:

Or use this link:

Jessica Jackson Writer

Or within Facebook, type into the search bar:

Jessica Jackson Writer

Can We Prevent These Murders?

There are no easy solutions, but these are my own views, which I cover in the pages of my books, echoing the advice of the World Health Organisation (WHO).

1 - End physical discipline of children

2 - Regulate homeschooling effectively

3 - An outlet for caregivers' anger

4 - Listen to the children when they report abuse

5 - Improve communication between agencies

6 - Safe places for unwanted babies

7 - Educate the parents of the future:
- that a baby communicates by crying
- how to give love, safety and guidance
- about bladder & bowel habits of children

In an ideal world, children would not be brought into an environment where drugs and/or violence abound, or where they are unwanted, or are wanted only to meet the impossible-to-meet needs of a parent. But to protect the ones who are already born, we need adequate support, education and a joined-up system where an abused child does not fall through the cracks.

Warning Signs of Abuse

There are various factors that might suggest a child is being abused. This list has been compiled by the NSPCC, but is by no means exhaustive:

- unexplained changes in behaviour or personality

- becoming withdrawn or anxious

- becoming uncharacteristically aggressive

- lacking social skills and having few friends

- poor bonding or relationship with a parent

- knowledge of adult issues inappropriate for their age

- running away or going missing

- wearing clothes which cover their body

And I would add:

- marks and bruises on the body

- being secretive

- stealing (often food)

- weight loss

- inappropriate clothing

- poor hygiene / unkempt appearance

- tiredness

- inability to concentrate

- being overly eager to please the adult

- the child telling you that they're being hurt

- a non-verbal child showing you that they're being hurt
- the adult removing the child from school after they have come under suspicion

If you suspect an adult of abusing a child, don't unquestioningly accept what they say, but instead:

A - Assume nothing

B - Be vigilant

C - Check everything

D - Do something

Listen to the children and report what you see:

TO REPORT CHILD ABUSE IN THE USA & CANADA

The National Child Abuse Hotline:1-800-422-4453
If a child is in immediate danger, call 911

TO REPORT CHILD ABUSE IN THE UK

For adults, call the NSPCC on 0808 800 5000
For children, call Childline on 0800 1111
Or if there is risk of imminent danger, ring 999

TO REPORT CHILD ABUSE IN AUSTRALIA

The National Child Abuse Reportline: 131-478
Children, call: 1800-55-1800
If a child is in immediate danger, call 000

Find All My Books on Amazon

Find them in your usual way, or you can …

Search Amazon for:

Abused To Death by Jessica Jackson

Or scan this code:

Or use this link:

https://viewbook.at/abused-series

I'd love you to **Follow** me on Amazon too!

Don't Miss A Thing

Pick up your free ebook:

Just scan this code:

https://BookHip.com/KXACJDT

Follow me on Facebook:

Jessica Jackson Writer

Follow me on Amazon:

https://author.to/jessicajackson

*(Ensure your Settings in **Communications / Preferences in Amazon** are set to receive info about new releases.)*

Selected Resources

Because She Loves You
Charmaine West,
Gloucester, UK
aged 8
Died 1971

Rose West: The Making of a Monster
Jane Carter Woodrow, Hodder & Stoughton Ltd 2001

Fred & Rose West: The Real Story
Hosted by Sir Trevor McDonald, ITV documentary - 2019

Fred & Rose: The Full Story of Fred and Rose West
Howard Sounes - Sphere - 05.09.11

Two Weddings and a Funeral
Daniel Valerio
Victoria, Australia
aged 2
Died 1990

Killing Daniel, from True Stories
Helen Garner,The Text Publishing Company - 2017

Mother of Daniel Valerio lashes abuse failure
Georgie Pilcher, news.co.au - 16.08.09

Daniel Valerio's killer free after 19 years
Mariza O'Keefe, The Courier Mail - 14.01.11

The Cage
Christian Choate
Indiana, USA
aged 13
Died 2009

Accused couple's bail petition dismissed
From Chicago Post Tribune - huffpost.com - 20.12.11

Father who tortured, killed son: 'I have nightmares'
Brad Edwards - chicago.cbslocal.com - 29.10.13

Kimberly Kubina v State of Indiana Court of Appeal
Judge Bailey - caselaw.findlaw.com - 06.11.13

Neighbours
Ayesha Ali
London, UK
aged 8
Died 2013

'Narcissist' Kiki Muddar will not give evidence
barkinganddagenhampost.co.uk - 05.02.15

Ayesha Ali killing: Mother and lover found guilty
bbc.co.uk - 04.03.15

Mother who tortured & killed eight-year-old daughter jailed for 13 years
theguardian.com - 06.03.15

The Best of Everything
Omaree Varela
New Mexico, USA
aged 9
Died 2013

Synthia Varela-Casaus: Meth 'became her life'
Rick Nathanson, Albuquerque Journal - 06.04.14

The Tragic Case of Omaree Varela
Barbara Alvarez, HuffPost - 27.08.14

Full 911 Call (Updated) Omaree Varela Case 2013
Court on Crime, Youtube - 20.08.18

Nobody's Child
Lauren Wright
Herts, UK
aged 6
Died 2000

Everyone saw Lauren suffering but no-one saved her
Sally Pook - telegraph.co.uk - 02.10.01

Executive Summary of Serious Case Review - Lauren Wright
Norfolk Area Child Protection Committee - 2001

Lack of safeguards for Lauren
news.bbc.co.uk - 27.03.02

The Good Student
Abdifatah
Mohamud
Buffalo, USA
aged 10
Died 2012

'I don't want to go back with him'.
Lou Michel - buffnews.com - 19.04.12

'I'm being abused': Abdifatah Mohamud to 911 operator in 2011
Lou Michel - buffnews.com - 25.04.12

Why did nobody save him?
Rachel Quigley - dailymail.com - 26.04.12

A Matter of Inexperience
PJ Bourgeois
Ohio, USA
aged 3
Died 1996

'I remember the moment that I first saw human bite marks'
Bob Greene - Jewish World Review - 05.10.00

'He wouldn't eat his eggs, and we put him to bed'
Bob Greene - Jewish World Review - 11.10.00

Blaming the boy for bringing on his own killing
Bob Greene - Jewish World Review - 23.10.00

Easy Review Codes

It's quick & easy – just a star rating
or a few words is all it takes

For Amazon.com
(US, NZ, SA, etc)

For Amazon in the UK

For Amazon in Canada

For Amazon in Australia

Or find it in your usual way

Thank you very much x

Disclaimer

My aim in writing this series is to tell the children's stories with a combination of accuracy and readability, and to heighten awareness of child torture and murder, and to explore ways of preventing further tragedies. I have relied on the factual information available to me during my research. Where I have added characters or dramatised events to better tell the stories, I believe I have done so without significantly altering the important details. If anyone has further information about any of the cases, I would be happy to hear from them. Likewise, if I have unwittingly quoted when I was not at liberty to do so, please get in touch so that this can be rectified.

Whilst every attempt has been made to make contact with copyright holders, where this has not been possible, I would be happy to be contacted by the relevant people, on: **jessicajackson@jesstruecrime.com** – thank you.

Printed in Dunstable, United Kingdom